Prayers
Before the
Bell

Inviting Christ
Into the Classroom

BETTY MANION

Liguori

Imprimi Potest
Harry Grile, CSsR, Provincial
Denver Province, The Redemptorists

Published by Liguori Publications
Liguori, Missouri 63057
To order, call 800-325-9521
www.liguori.org

Library of Congress Cataloging-in-Publication Data

Manion, Betty.
  Prayers before the bell : inviting Christ into the classroom / Betty Manion.
-- 1st ed.
     p. cm.
  ISBN 978-0-7648-2146-2
  1. Students--Prayers and devotions. 2. Prayer--Christianity. I. Title.
  BV4531.3.M353 2012
  242'.62--dc23
                    2012001053

Compliant with *The Roman Missal,* third edition.

Scripture quotations are from *New Revised Standard Version Bible,* copyright © 1989 National Council of the Churches of Christ in the United States of America. Used by permission. All rights reserved.

Liguori Publications, a nonprofit corporation, is an apostolate of the Redemptorists. To learn more about the Redemptorists, visit Redemptorists.com.

Printed in the United States of America
16 15 14 13 12 / 5 4 3 2
First Edition

Dedicated to my parents, who taught me how to pray with words and showed me how to pray by their actions.

Contents

Introduction

Praying with children is one of the most profound experiences an adult can have, perhaps because children pray so differently. Adults tend to beat around the bush with God. We might be afraid or feel we're unworthy. We aren't as honest as we could be. Children come forward fearlessly. Their words are direct and heartfelt. They bring honesty, sincerity, self-confidence, and wonder into their prayer.

This book helps parents, teachers, and catechists give students a structured moment of prayer each day of the school year. Ideally, the week could unfold as follows:

DAY 1   CLASSROOM PRAYER SERVICE

▼ Discussion question to prompt students to share their thoughts

▼ Scripture passage to highlight or illustrate the theme

▼ Prayer

DAY 2   PRAYER

DAY 3   PRAYER

DAY 4   PRAYER

DAY 5   PRAYER

Bishop Robert Morneau of the Diocese of Green Bay refers to the purposes of prayer as "whoops, wow, thanks, and help." I love his approach, and the prayers in this book echo this pattern.

I hope you find this book to be a concise and convenient resource for use in Catholic schools, religious-education classes, other faith traditions, or any forum for prayer with young people. I also hope its simple style will lead children into their own experiences of prayer. Most important, may it help you welcome Christ into your classroom.

Betty Manion

Inviting Christ Into the Classroom

Lord Jesus,
we invite you into our classroom today.
Bless our minds and fill them with knowledge
and wonder about your world.
Bless our hands as they become your hands
of care and thoughtfulness to others.
Open our eyes to all
our education offers us each day,
and help us learn your ways.
Fill our mouths with kind words
that show appreciation to our teachers,
classmates, and friends.
Forgive us when we forget that you are our guest.
Thank you for dwelling in our hearts, our classroom,
and our school with your spirit, grace, and love.
May we serve you with our learning
and love what we do in your name.
We ask all of this through you,
our greatest teacher of all. Amen.

Section One

We Are God's Family

WEEK 1

New Beginnings

What will you do to begin this school year walking in love?

2 JOHN 1:4–6

I was overjoyed to find some of your children walking in the truth just as we have been commanded by the Father. But now...I ask you, not as though I were writing you a new commandment, but one we have found from the beginning, let us love one another. And this is love, that we walk according to his commandments; this is the commandment just as you have heard it from the beginning—you must walk in it.

DAY 1

Loving God, we thank you for the gift of this school year.
Help us always appreciate the opportunity to learn
and the gift of gathering at a school,
a gift not available to every child.
May we never take our education for granted
and never complain about school.
Help us do our best
with all you've given us to learn this year.
We ask this through Jesus,
who always did his best. Amen.

DAY 2

Dear Jesus, bless our school, our teachers,
our classrooms, and the students
so our school will be a place of learning and love.
Help our teachers do their best
and guide us to be the best students possible.
May our classrooms be places of hospitality,
compassion, excitement, blessings, and joy.
May our minds and our hearts be filled with knowledge
of you, our world, and all that will
help us grow in faith with you.
We ask this through your Son,
the greatest teacher and student of all. Amen.

DAY 3

Dear Jesus, new beginnings give us a time to make new friends.
You taught us that friendship means
caring for others with our heart and soul.
Help us treasure our old friends
as we reach out to those we don't know.
Help us see that each of us is your child,
filled with your very special gifts.

Help us use our gifts and recognize and honor
the gifts of our friends, new and old.
We ask this through you,
our God who is ever ancient, ever new. Amen.

DAY 4

Dear God, how wonderful it must be to know all things!
Help us gain as much knowledge
as we can about you and your world.
Fill our minds with wonder
about all we don't know, and
help us be excited about all we will learn.
May we be humble about our abilities
and never be know-it-alls.
Thank you for the example of your son, Jesus,
who did know it all but never bragged about it. Amen.

DAY 5

Dear Lord, a new year means new opportunities
for us to grow as leaders.
Help us be leaders in our classrooms,
leaders in our school, and leaders in our world.
Leaders are wise, patient, and compassionate
and speak up for others.
Jesus was the perfect leader.
Guide our minds and hearts to act as he did.
Help us see every moment
we can be a leader for you,
where we can act with love and kindness to all. Amen.

Be Who God Made You to Be

How can you use your talents to help your school or family?

ADAPTED FROM MATTHEW 25:14–26

A man who was going on a journey called his servants. To one he gave five talents, to another two, and to a third he gave one talent. Then he went away. The servant with five talents used them to make five more talents. The one with two talents made two more talents. But the one with one talent dug a hole and buried it. When the master returned, the one with the five talents come forward with the five more. "Well done!" said the Master. The one with the two talents came forward and handed over the two more. "Well done!" said the Master. Then the one with the one talent said, "I was afraid, so I dug a hole and buried your talent in the ground. Here, it is yours." But his Master replied, "You lazy servant."

DAY 1

Dear God, thank you for blessing each of us
with special gifts and talents.
May we be like the wise servants
who used their talents in the best way,
and not like the unwise servant
who buried his talent and never shared it.
Help us use our talents to love and serve you. Amen.

DAY 2

Loving Father, through our baptism
you call us to serve each other as your children.
Help us see that we must be the best
we can be so others
can be the best they can be.
This means following you in faith and love and service.
Thank you for welcoming us into your family.
May we always use the gifts
you have given us to serve you and others. Amen.

DAY 3

Dear Jesus, you were blessed with many talents.
You showed us your gift of peacemaking
by showing us how to love everyone.
You showed us your gift of compassion
by caring for those who have less than we do.
You showed us your gift of preaching
by teaching us about faith and love.
And you showed us your gift of mercy
by forgiving all who made mistakes.
Thank you for teaching us how to share
your gifts with others.
May we never disappoint you. Amen.

DAY 4

Dear Holy Spirit, through you we are inspired
to be the best we can be.
Open our eyes to help us see our abilities
and each other's gifts.
Help us never disrespect the gifts
God has given us
and to never be jealous of others' abilities.
May we never take our gifts for granted,
and may we always remember to share them with others.
We ask this through Jesus, who shared his life with us. Amen.

DAY 5

Creator God, you began a good work in each of us.
Help us know our gifts,
deepen our understanding of them,
develop them, and share them with others.
If we do this in faith, we can
help you continue the masterpiece
of your kingdom on Earth.
As we use our gifts, guide us
to be your unique servant.
We ask this through Jesus,
your gift to the world. Amen.

The Greatest Commandments

*What does it mean to love someone in the
same way you love yourself?*

MATTHEW 22:34-40

*They gathered together, and one of them, a lawyer, asked him
a question to test him. "Teacher, which commandment in the
law is the greatest?" He said to him, 'You shall love the Lord
your God with all your heart, and with all your soul, and with
all your mind.' This is the greatest and first commandment.
And a second is like it: 'You shall love your neighbor as yourself.' On these two commandments hang all the law and the
prophets.*

DAY 1

Dear Father, you call us to love our
neighbor as we love ourselves
and to treat others as we would like to be treated.
Fill our hearts with your goodness
so our actions become second nature
and bring us closer to you.
We ask this through Jesus, who is love for all. Amen.

DAY 2

Dear heavenly Father, you made your world out of love.
We are sorry for when we fail to appreciate
all you have done for us.
Thank you for sending your son, Jesus,
to guide us to the right path and show us how to live.
May his example always remind us
that we are to love you above *all* things
and love our neighbor
just as much as we love ourselves.
We ask this through your Son,
our model of love. Amen.

DAY 3

Dear loving Jesus, you taught us that love
is stronger than anything on Earth.
Thank you for showing us that by
keeping God first and honoring him
with our words and actions,
we are keeping your first great commandment.
Thank you for showing us that
when we put the needs of our neighbor first,
we show your love and
live your second great commandment.
Help us see that these are our pathway to heaven. Amen.

DAY 4

Dear Holy Spirit, through you
we learn that we can reach out
in love to one another.
Open our eyes to see not only what is important to us,
but how we are connected to everyone around us.
Help us see the needs of others
in our classrooms, on the playground,
in our families, and throughout the whole world. Amen.

Gracious God, you teach us
to love one another through your works of mercy.
Mercy is reaching out to others with compassion.
Open our hearts to recognize moments
when we can feed, shelter, clothe, comfort,
mend, tend, visit, and listen to others' needs.
Thank you for your son, Jesus, who showed us
that love really makes a difference.
Help us go forth and make a difference for you. Amen.

WEEK 4

We Are Church

What does Jesus mean by "a faith built on sand"?

MATTHEW 7:24–27

Everyone then who hears these words of mine and acts on them will be like a wise man who built his house on rock. The rain fell, the floods came, and the winds blew and beat on that house, but it did not fall, because it had been founded on rock. And everyone who hears these words of mine and does not act on them will be like a foolish man who built his house on sand. The rain fell, and the floods came, and the winds blew and beat against that house, and it fell—and great was its fall!

DAY 1

Dear Jesus, you taught us
that the way to God is through you.
Thank you for being our rock.
You loved us so much that you gave your life for us.
You proved nothing is impossible for you!
Help our faith be like you: solid and steadfast like a rock.
We ask this through you,
who rolled away the rock of your tomb just for us. Amen.

DAY 2

Dear heavenly Father, you are the cornerstone
of our faith, the rock of all ages.
Thank you for always being there for us.
Fill us with your Spirit
so we can deepen our understanding of you
through the teachings of our Church,
the lives of the saints,
the words of Scripture,
and the long tradition of our Catholic faith.
May we always seek to learn more about you
and be living signs of your Church. Amen.

DAY 3

Loving Jesus, you taught us to
build our faith on you, our rock.
Deepen our faith to be like a rock
so that nothing is chipped away when challenges come,
especially when we're tempted to make anything
more important than you.
We ask this through you,
who resisted all temptation. Amen.

DAY 4

Dear Holy Spirit, we ask that you strengthen our Church
and guide our leaders to make good decisions
for all your people.
Bless our pope, our cardinals, our bishops, our priests,
and all who help lead us to you.
Bless us so we may always serve you,
and unite us so we may all grow
in love for you and for one another.
We ask this in love. Amen.

DAY 5

Dear Father, thank you for being the rock
and foundation of our faith.
Like rock, may we be strong for others.
When they struggle,
when things are difficult,
when we don't know what to do,
may we hold firmly to our faith
and hope in you.
Anchor our faith so we can join you one day
in your heavenly kingdom. Amen.

We Are One in Christ

WEEK 5

Faith

*Is it ever hard for you to have
faith in God? Why?*

LUKE 12:22–34

*[Jesus] said..."Therefore I tell you, do not worry about your
life, what you will eat, or about your body, what you will
wear....Consider the ravens: they neither sow nor reap, they
have neither storehouse nor barn, and yet God feeds them....
Consider the lilies, how they grow: they neither toil nor spin;
yet I tell you, even Solomon in all his glory was not clothed like
one of these. [S]trive for his kingdom, and these things will be
given to you as well."*

DAY 1

Dear God, you've given
the beautiful gift of faith to each of us.
Help us welcome that gift and trust in you.
When we're troubled, when we're afraid,
when we're uncertain, or when we're worried,
help us trust that you will be with us
as you are with the birds and the flowers.
Thank you for your endless love.
We ask this in the name of Jesus,
who taught us to have faith in you. Amen.

DAY 2

Dear Lord, we must put ourselves in your hands.
Help us have faith to know that you will always be with us
and listen to our prayers.
When we place our trust completely in you,
we realize that your love for us is beyond measure.
Fill us with faith in you. Amen.

DAY 3

Dear Lord, sometimes it's hard to believe in things
we cannot see,
yet that is what faith calls us to do.
How can we ever doubt your love
and concern for all your children?
When we lose faith,
help us see your presence everywhere—
in the air we breathe, the food we eat,
the families we love, and the friends who support us.
We ask this through Jesus,
who has faith in each of us. Amen.

DAY 4

Dear Lord, throughout all ages,
people have turned from you and put faith in false things.
When we are wrapped up in ourselves,
help us be faithful to you.
When we make things more important than you,
help us be faithful to you.
When we doubt your presence,
help us be faithful to you.
You alone are the source of faith.
Thank you for never losing faith in us. Amen.

DAY 5

Dear Lord, sometimes it's hard to find you.
When we have trouble in our families, we look for you.
When those we love become ill, we look for you.
When our friends desert us, we look for you.
When tragedy hits, we look for you.
When we feel lonely, we look for you.
During all these times, fill us with faith in you—
faith that comforts us and lets us know
you're with us at all times,
holding us in your loving care. Amen.

Hope

What are your hopes for yourself, our school,
and our world?

LAMENTATIONS 3:22–26

The steadfast love of the LORD never ceases, his mercies never come to an end; they are new every morning; great is your faithfulness. "The LORD is my portion," says my soul, "therefore I will hope in him." The LORD is good to those who wait for him, to the soul that seeks him. It is good that one should wait quietly for the salvation of the LORD.

DAY 1

Heavenly Father, you're the source of all hope.
You're the opposite of despair.
With our lives centered in you,
we look forward to joining you in heaven.
Just as the prophets called people
to lives filled with goodness,
you call us to live in goodness.
May we always be faithful to you,
especially during difficult times.
We ask this of you,
through whom all things are possible. Amen.

DAY 2

Dear Jesus, give us the strength
to remain children of hope.
When things go wrong, make us strong.
When people we love are ill or die, or
when we try hard and fail,
fill us with the hope
that comes from knowing God has a plan for us.
When we feel like giving up, hold us in your care and
let us know you're always with us
no matter what. Amen.

DAY 3

Dear Jesus, when you faced your
suffering and death on the cross,
you asked your Father for strength to do his will.
You never gave up, and you knew
he would help you through your suffering.
Help us never give up.
When we are tired, discouraged, or sad,
hold us up so we can trust in you.
We ask this through you,
our greatest source of hope. Amen.

DAY 4

Dear Lord, why do some people
have more problems than others?
Help us see all our blessings,
and help us bring hope to others.
Our friendship, our kind deeds, and our words
can bring *you* to those in need.
We ask this through you,
who helps carry our burdens. Amen.

Dear Jesus, through your resurrection you conquered despair
and won heaven for all who believe in you.
Thank you for never giving up
and for seeing God's plan through to the end.
Thank you for your glorious resurrection,
which gives us ultimate hope
that we'll join you in eternal happiness.
No matter how tough life gets, we know
we'll someday be happy with you in heaven. Amen.

WEEK 7

Love

What do you love best about God?

ROMANS 8:35, 38–39

Who will separate us from the love of Christ? Will hardship, or distress, or persecution, or famine, or nakedness, or peril, or sword?...For I am convinced that neither death, nor life, nor angels, nor rulers, nor things present, nor things to come, nor powers, nor height, nor depth, nor anything else in all creation, will be able to separate us from the love of God in Christ Jesus our Lord.

DAY 1

God of all love,
help us always believe in your love,
and help us know that nothing
we could ever do will make you love us less.
Help us remember that when we love others,
we are one with you.
We ask this through Jesus, our brother,
who showed us how to love completely. Amen.

DAY 2

Dear Lord, how can we begin to know your love?
Perhaps the best way is to see the beauty of the world
you created just for us.
You filled it with mountains and oceans,
sunsets and sunrises, trees and flowers,
animals and amphibians—all things that show
how great you are.
Thank you for our world,
which reveals your immense love for us.
Help us always care for your creation
as a sign of our love for you. Amen.

DAY 3

Dear Father, we are part of your family of love.
Help us know that the more love we give away,
the more love we receive.
Teach us to love more completely
by putting others' needs before our own.
Help us love our neighbor
even when it might be hard.
Help us see Jesus in every person we meet.
We ask this through Jesus, who taught us
to love our neighbor as we love ourselves. Amen.

DAY 4

Dear God, sometimes we find love
in the most surprising places
and at the most surprising times.
Help us see those blessed moments
when your love shines through
the kindness of a neighbor, the concern of a teacher,
the compassion of a classmate—all moments of your love.
Help us be agents of your love.
Fill us with the gifts to let your love shine through us.
We ask this through Jesus,
who loved everyone he met. Amen.

DAY 5

Loving Father, thank you for loving us so completely.
You teach us that love is patient and kind,
generous and compassionate,
and that it is never rude or boastful.
Sometimes it's hard to love like that.
When others are difficult to love,
help us see them through your eyes.
When we're difficult to love,
help others see you in us.
Thank you for the example of Jesus,
who showed us how to love without judging.
We ask your help in this mission of love. Amen.

Discipleship

When is it hard to be a disciple of Jesus?

MATTHEW 10:5–11

These twelve Jesus sent out with the following instructions: "Go...to the lost sheep of the house of Israel. As you go, proclaim the good news, 'The kingdom of heaven has come near.' Cure the sick, raise the dead, cleanse the lepers, cast out demons. You received without payment; give without payment. Take no gold, or silver, or copper in your belts, no bag for your journey, or two tunics, or sandals, or a staff; for laborers deserve their food."

DAY 1

Dear Jesus, you called your disciples
to leave everything behind
and go forth to teach about you.
That was very hard to do,
but they did it because they believed in you
and loved you so much.
May our actions tell others that we are your disciples. Amen.

DAY 2

Dear Jesus, your disciples were ordinary men
who did all they could
to carry out your mission on Earth.
Sometimes we wonder why you call on us, Lord—
we who are imperfect disciples.
Give us what we need to be able to serve you well.
Help us overcome our doubts and fears
so we can be your true disciples. Amen.

DAY 3

Dear Jesus, to be a true disciple means
to humble ourselves and serve others.
Jesus, you say we achieve greatness
only through serving our neighbor.
Help us do what we can to help others.
Open our eyes to everyone around us
so we might be called your disciples. Amen.

DAY 4

Dear Jesus, your light shines through those who serve you.
Help us shine!
Sometimes we want to do our will instead of yours.
Help us put our lives in your hands
so we can truly do your work.
We ask this through you who emptied yourself for us. Amen.

DAY 5

Dear Jesus, when you were on Earth,
you cared for the poor, you loved everyone,
you taught us about faith in your Father,
and you forgave others.
Lord, help us speak kind words in our classrooms,
forgive those who hurt us, be kind to everyone,
and show our faith by our words and actions.
Thank you, Lord, for your example. Amen.

The Body of Christ

What happens if one or two parts of the Body of Christ are missing?

ADAPTED FROM 1 CORINTHIANS 12:12–20

As the body is one and it has many members, and all the members of the body, though many, are one body, so it is with Christ. Indeed one body does not consist of one member, but of many. If the foot would say, "Because I am not a hand, I do not belong to the body," or if the ear would say, "Because I am not an eye, I do not belong to the body," that would not make them any less a part of the body....The eye cannot say to the hand, "I have no need of you."...As it is, there are many members, but only one body.

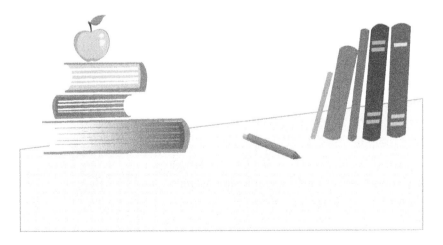

DAY 1

Dear Jesus, you taught us that each of us is unique,
yet we are the same, because we are all children of God.
May we be like you and love everyone—
all the parts of the Body of Christ.
Help us know that when we love others,
we actually love you.
Fill us with your love as we
seek to be your Body here on Earth. Amen.

DAY 2

Dear heavenly Father, we thank you for your son, Jesus,
who teaches us to love as you do.
Help us not worry about what someone else
is or isn't doing, and help us not judge their actions.
Instead, help us stay centered in you,
focused on how we can serve you and others.
Make us the best we can be
so we can help build your kingdom on Earth. Amen.

DAY 3

Dear loving Jesus, sometimes things go wrong
and we are ill or injured.
Sometimes things go wrong in the Body of Christ.
Lord, help us bring healing
when our members are hurt or in pain.
Help us mend disagreements between our members.
Help us always act with justice, compassion, and peace.
We ask this through you who are peace. Amen.

DAY 4

Dear Holy Spirit, we praise you
as the wisdom and life of our Church.
Fill us with your Spirit, so that with Jesus
we may live as the Body of Christ.
Help us see that we should value
the *whole* Body of Christ
and not just our part of the Body.
Help us care for all members of the Body.
We ask this through Jesus, who cared for *all* of us. Amen.

DAY 5

Dear Jesus, as members of the Body of Christ,
we're called to see *you* in everyone.
Lord, help us understand that we see you
when we see someone in need.
When someone is lonely, help us comfort.
When someone is sad, help us console.
When someone needs a friend, help us be a friend.
Thank you for teaching us that what we do for others,
we do for you. Amen.

Autumn

WEEK 10

Communion of Saints

Do you have a favorite saint? Who is it? Why?

1 THESSALONIANS 4:13–14, 16, 18

But we do not want you to be uninformed, brothers and sisters, about those who have died, so that you may not grieve as others do who have no hope. For since we believe that Jesus died and rose again, even so, through Jesus, God will bring with him those who have died....For the Lord himself, with a cry of command, with the archangel's call and with the sound of God's trumpet, will descend from heaven, and the dead in Christ will rise first. Then we who are alive, who are left, will be caught up in the clouds together with them to meet the Lord in the air; and so we will be with the Lord for ever. Therefore encourage one another with these words.

DAY 1

Dear Father, thank you for the gift of the saints.
Help us live our faith just as they did.
Help us use our hearts, minds, and bodies
to love and serve you and one another.
Teach us to see you in all things as they did.
By learning about the saints, we can learn about
bravery, humility, faith, love, compassion,
and total faith in you.
Guide us as we imitate them.
We ask this through you,
our best example of how to be a saint.
Amen.

DAY 2

Dear saints, you didn't give up your faith in God
even when life was hard or when sickness, poverty,
or hardship came your way.
Instead, you continued to love and praise God.
When problems come, help us never give up.
When people are suffering, help us be there
to comfort them as you did.
Even the littlest actions can help:
Mother Teresa said we can do small things with great love.
May we do so with her help and the help of Jesus,
through whom we make this prayer. Amen.

DAY 3

Dear saints of God, it takes much courage
to defend something.
You stood up for your faith,
supported your brothers and sisters,
and defended our heavenly Father.
When we must enter battles for what is right and wrong,

help us have the strength of Saints Joan and Michael.
When we must stand up for something we believe in,
make us strong.
When others are weak, help us defend them.
May we always be a voice
for those who can't speak for themselves.
We humbly pray. Amen.

DAY 4

Dear holy men and women, you prayed *all* the time.
You knew that praying brings us close to God.
Saint Benedict told us that our lives
should be about working and praying.
Help us do our school work, our homework,
and our housework the best way we can.
Help us pray often and well by honoring God,
thanking God, and asking God for help.
We ask this through Jesus, who taught us to pray. Amen.

DAY 5

Heavenly saints of God, you knew what it was like to be
totally devoted to God and your neighbor.
You were selfless to your own needs
and dedicated to the needs of others.
Like Saint Francis, you knew that in giving, we receive.
Help us be aware of others' needs.
Help us share what we have
so all people have what they need.
When someone needs our help, may we give it freely.
When someone needs a friend, let us be a friend.
Then we will know how good it feels to live like you.
We ask this through you. Amen.

Respect Life: Creation

Did you ever make something for someone?
Was it appreciated?

GENESIS 1:26–28, 30–31

So God created humankind in his image,...male and female he created them. God blessed them, and God said to them, "Be fruitful and multiply, and fill the earth and subdue it; and have dominion over the fish of the sea and over the birds of the air and over every living thing that moves upon the earth...." And it was so. God saw everything that he had made, and indeed, it was very good.

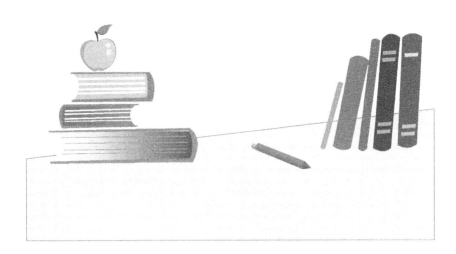

DAY 1

Dear Father, thank you
for the gift of our wonderful world.
We know it's a sign of your love.
For the long-necked giraffes that make us laugh
and the giant elephants that amaze us, we honor you.
For the beautiful butterflies that fill the air
and the colorful rainbows that fill our skies, we honor you.
Help us always treasure this Earth
and be its best caretakers.
We honor and praise you for the wonder you are.
In humble thanks, we pray. Amen.

DAY 2

Dear Lord, we know life is fragile.
Each of us is a unique creation.
You love each of us as your child.
Thank you for loving us in such a special way.
May we always view each other as your special children.
May we see your presence in everyone we meet.
Help us treat one another as you treat us.
We ask this through your Holy Spirit, your breath of life. Amen.

DAY 3

Dear Jesus, through your life,
you taught us how to respect all life.
You showed us that young and old, male and female,
Jew or Samaritan, blind or paralyzed, we are all special to you.
Help us see as you do.
Help us never judge the value of another life
as anything but good, complete, and whole.
Help us treat every person with dignity and respect.
May we be a voice for those who cannot speak for themselves.
May we praise you with our lives
until we take our last breath. Amen.

DAY 4

Dear Lord, when you created our world,
you allowed us to become its caretakers.
It's ours to cherish and pass on to those who come after us.
Help us see how we can make a difference.
When we turn off lights, we care for your world;
when we recycle, we care for your world;
when we don't litter, we care for your world;
when we compost, we care for your world.
Help us see that every little thing we do
shows our love and respect for you, our creator.
Thank you for all we have and for all you are. Amen.

DAY 5

Dear Jesus, sometimes it's hard to respect others.
When someone is unkind to us,
may we respect them by not getting angry.
When someone hurts us,
may we respect them by forgiving them.
When someone is selfish and won't share,
may we respect them by being polite.
Thank you for teaching us to be kind,
because when we harm others we harm ourselves.
We are all part of your creation.
Help us care for one another and for our world. Amen.

WEEK 12

The Rosary

Is it sometimes easier for you to talk to your mother than to your father? Why?

LUKE 1:39–42

In those days Mary set out and went with haste to a Judean town in the hill country, where she entered the house of Zechariah and greeted Elizabeth. When Elizabeth heard Mary's greeting, the child leapt in her womb. And Elizabeth was filled with the Holy Spirit and exclaimed with a loud cry, "Blessed are you among women, and blessed is the fruit of your womb."

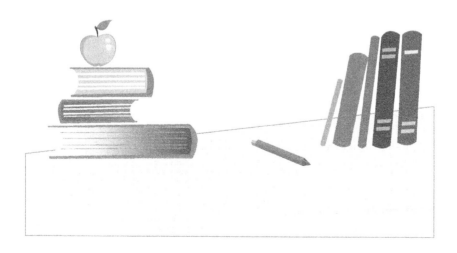

DAY 1

Dear Jesus, thank you for the gift of your mother, Mary.
May we always treasure her as you do.
Help us live as she did in devotion to you.
May her example of motherly love
teach us to love completely.
Just as she lived in devotion to you,
may we live in devotion to you and others.
May our actions make her
proud to be our heavenly mother.
Keep us safe until we meet you and her in heaven. Amen.

DAY 2

Dear Mary, your life was filled
with many sorrowful moments
as you watched your Son suffer for us.
When we're sad, help us be strong like you.
When things happen that don't make sense,
help us understand as you did.
When things don't go our way,
help us accept it as you did.
May we always feel your heavenly arms
comforting us in our sorrow. Amen.

DAY 3

Dear Mary, just as some moments
brought you great joy,
we too have joyful moments.
Help us never take these moments for granted.
Help us always see them as gifts from your Son.
Never let us forget to thank God for them.
Help us see that joyful moments
bring us closer to you and Jesus.
When we endure sad times,
let the memory of our joyful moments give us hope. Amen.

DAY 4

Dear Mary, how blessed you were to have glorious moments.
Help us see our own joyful moments as glimpses of heaven.
We give thanks for the glorious resurrection of your Son,
who was victorious in the battle of good and evil.
We give thanks for the gift of the Holy Spirit,
who will guide us to the glorious day
we join you in eternal life. Amen.

DAY 5

Dear Mary, through the rosary
we can honor the wonderful events in your life.
Help us be aware of moments
that can change our lives and bring us closer to your Son.
May we always have faith in Jesus as you did at Cana.
May we realize that the gift of the Eucharist nourishes us
and lights the way for us to be disciples of Christ.
Help us always see that you and your Son
light our path to holiness. Amen.

Feasts of All Saints and All Souls

What in today's Scripture gives you comfort?

JOHN 14:1–7

"Do not let your hearts be troubled. Believe in God, believe also in me. In my Father's house there are many dwelling-places....And if I go and prepare a place for you, I will come again and will take you to myself....I am the way, and the truth, and the life. No one comes to the Father except through me. If you know me, you will know my Father also."

DAY 1

Dear Jesus, you give us comfort about death
and tell us what to expect in heaven.
Thank you for winning heaven for us
and for your words of eternal life.
They give us hope and guidance for
living with you forever in heaven.
Thank you for showing how much you love us
by preparing a place for us.
Help us follow your ways so that, through you,
we can come to your Father. Amen.

DAY 2

Dear Jesus, we're so sad when someone we love dies.
We can't imagine how we'll live without them.
During those sad times, fill our hearts with your peace
so we can be happy for the person we miss,
knowing they're safe in your care.
Comfort us in our sorrow, Lord,
and let the wonderful memories fill our hearts with joy. Amen.

DAY 3

Dear Jesus, you promise us the kingdom of heaven
if we believe in you and follow your ways.
Sometimes we're not good at doing this.
Give us a strong faith
so we can see your presence in times of doubt.
Fill us with joy beyond our sadness or anger,
and give us the comfort only you can give
when someone we love is gone.
Be with us in our sorrow until we join you
in our heavenly home. Amen.

DAY 4

Dear Jesus, saints show us how to live.
By following their lives in faith,
we too can become saints on Earth.
Help us be examples of love.
Help us show respect for our neighbor and for you.
Above all, we humbly ask to be happy
with them and you in heaven. Amen.

Dear Jesus, sometimes we don't appreciate people
until they're gone. Lord, help us do better.
Fill us with appreciation for everyone we meet.
Help us appreciate the gifts they are.
Help us appreciate our family members
and those who take care of us.
Open our lips to speak words of love and appreciation.
Help us never take them for granted.
We ask this through you who bless us daily. Amen.

WEEK 14

Thanksgiving

What blessings are you most grateful for?

1 THESSALONIANS 5:14–18

And we urge you, beloved, to admonish the idlers, encourage the faint-hearted, help the weak, be patient with all of them. See that none of you repays evil for evil, but always seek to do good to one another and to all. Rejoice always, pray without ceasing, give thanks in all circumstances; for this is the will of God in Christ Jesus for you.

DAY 1

Good and gracious God,
we gather in thanksgiving
for the abundant blessings you bestow.
We cannot even begin to understand your love,
but the many blessings you give
help us see the mystery of your grace.
Help us never take these gifts for granted.
Help us stop and thank you each day for what we have.
Help us be generous when we share our blessings,
as generous as you are with us.
We ask this through Jesus, who always gave you praise. Amen.

DAY 2

God of all creation,
you've given us a world filled with beauty
and hearts to see the depth of your love for us.
We give you thanks for the sun and moon and stars.
We give you thanks for their light and warmth.
Thank you for clouds and rain and snow,
which help things grow.
Thank you for rainbows, a sign of your never-ending love.
May we always honor you as our creator and loving God. Amen.

DAY 3

Dear Jesus, you taught us to give
what can't be bought or sold—gifts of the heart.
Help us always give thanks for your gifts
of compassion, kindness, forgiveness, mercy, and grace.
Fill our hearts with your love
so we can share these gifts with others.
Thank you for this most important lesson in giving. Amen.

DAY 4

Dear God, you loved us so much
that you gave us special people
to love and care for us on Earth.
Thank you for family members who love us.
Thank you for parents and grandparents,
brothers and sisters and pets, aunts and uncles and cousins.
Thank you for school and parish families.
Thank you for teachers, principals, and classmates,
Church leaders and all who teach us about you.
Thank you for our community.
Thank you for friends, neighbors,
and community leaders who protect us.
May we always be responsible members
of our families, communities, and world. Amen.

DAY 5

Dear God, virtues are gifts from you.
We thank you for these gifts.
We thank you for the gift of courage to fight for freedom
and to believe in you and in our country.
We thank you for the gift of understanding
that helps us know you and our neighbors.
We thank you for the gifts of fortitude and strength
that help us to bear hardships and sadness.
Most of all, we thank you for *you,* our loving Father. Amen.

Angels

When have you been an angel to someone?

HEBREWS 1:10–14

And, "In the beginning, Lord, you founded the earth, and the heavens are the work of your hands; they will perish, but you remain; they will all wear out like clothing; like a cloak you will roll them up, and like clothing they will be changed. But you are the same, and your years will never end." But to which of the angels has he ever said, "Sit at my right hand until I make your enemies a footstool for your feet"? Are not all angels spirits in the divine service, sent to serve for the sake of those who are to inherit salvation?

DAY 1

Heavenly Father, you have created
glorious messengers to bring us hope in times of need.
For this, we thank you.
Help us always be open to the presence of angels.
They help us know that you never forget us
and that you're always watching out for us.
We look forward to the day we join your angels
in singing glory and praise to you. Amen.

DAY 2

Dear God, how much you must love us!
You gave each of us
a special angel to guard us.
Thank you for the *awesome* gift of angels.
May we live a life of faith in you
with our angel's help and guidance.
May we know we're never alone
with them always at our side.
Thank you for the love, protection,
and guidance of angels. Amen.

DAY 3

Dear Jesus, when you were in the desert for forty days
you were tempted by Satan,
but you never gave in because God sent his angels
to watch over and protect you.
When we're in difficult situations,
send your angels to guide us to good choices.
When we're making decisions,
send your angels to help us stop and think.
With angels at our side,
we can be strong like you. Amen.

DAY 4

Dear Lord, when you were baptized, the heavens opened,
angels came forth, and your Father said,
"This is my Son, the Beloved,
with whom I am well pleased."
It's amazing to think you were also pleased on our baptism day.
Help us always live out our baptismal promises
so you are proud of us.
Send your angels to hover when we need you
and to guide us as we serve you.
We ask this through Jesus, who pleases you the best. Amen.

DAY 5

Dear Jesus, angels are your divine helpers.
Many times *we* have opportunities to be your helpers.
When we see someone who needs a smile,
may we be an angel.
When a teacher or classmate needs help,
may we be an angel.
When we see someone who is lonely,
may we go to their side just as our angel comes to ours.
Open our eyes so we can be angel helpers for you.
We do this in thanksgiving for all you do for us. Amen.

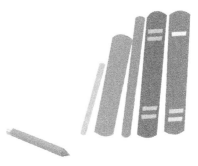

Advent ✤ Christmas

WEEK 16

Waiting

How can waiting be a good thing?

LAMENTATIONS 3:22–26

The steadfast love of the LORD never ceases, his mercies never come to an end; they are new every morning; great is your faithfulness. "The LORD is my portion," says my soul, "therefore I will hope in him." The LORD is good to those who wait for him, to the soul that seeks him. It is good that one should wait quietly for the salvation of the LORD.

DAY 1

Dear God, waiting is very hard for us.
We're used to getting things when we want them.
Help us be better at waiting.
Help us see how you wait for us *all* the time:
You wait for us to turn away from sin and follow you.
You wait for us to remember to say our prayers.
You wait for us to speak only words of kindness.
You wait for us to thank you for our blessings.
Thank you for being so patient with us.
Help us be patient too. Amen.

DAY 2

Lord, people waited thousands of years for the Savior.
Sometimes it feels that long when we wait for something.
Help us wait patiently this Advent for the gift of your Son.
Thank you for sending baby Jesus to light our world.
May we be a light to others this Advent.
We ask this through Jesus, the light of the world. Amen.

DAY 3

Dear Lord, patience is a virtue.
Patience eventually grows within us.
Help us become patient, Lord.
Calm our anxiousness.
When we have a hard time waiting our turn,
help us wait quietly.
When we're waiting in line, help us be courteous.
When we're learning new things,
help us be patient with ourselves.
Remind us, Lord, that you lived patiently.
Even when you were anxious, you were kind to everyone.
With your help, may we do the same. Amen.

DAY 4

Dear Lord, you told us heaven is a wonderful place
and that someday we'll be happy with you there.
Help us live every day in anticipation of heaven.
Help us realize that we're on a journey
to get closer to you each day.
Help us make the best of every day,
knowing each day is a chance to please you,
honor you, and grow in our faith with you.
If we love and follow you,
heaven will be worth the wait.
Thank you for loving us so much. Amen.

DAY 5

Dear Lord, your mother, Mary, had a long wait for you.
She was unsure of what was in store,
yet she waited with faith, putting her trust in you.
When we must wait,
help us wait as she did, in complete trust in you.
And when our waiting is done, help us accept
the outcome with grace, just as Mary did.
We ask this through you as we honor your mother,
who loves us and gave us you. Amen.

December Saints

Name ten things you're grateful for.

ISAIAH 9:2–3, 6

The people who walked in darkness have seen a great light; those who lived in a land of deep darkness—on them light has shined. You have multiplied the nation, you have increased its joy; they rejoice before you as with joy at the harvest, as people exult when dividing plunder. For the yoke of their burden, and the bar across their shoulders, the rod of their oppressor, you have broken as on the day of Midian. For all the boots of the tramping warriors and all the garments rolled in blood shall be burned as fuel for the fire. For a child has been born for us, a son given to us.

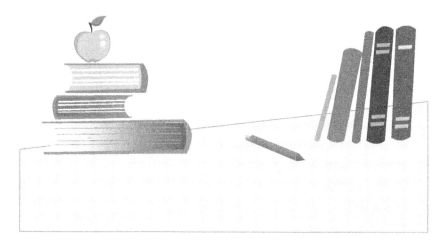

DAY 1

Dear Father in heaven, thank you
for the special month of December,
a month of bright starlight
and the month of the birth of your son, Jesus,
the light of the world.
Thank you for saints Lucy, Nicholas,
Juan Diego, and Our Lady of Guadalupe.
Through their example, we can be better servants
and grow closer to you.
Fill our hearts with December starlight
and the light of baby Jesus
so we can shine for others. Amen.

DAY 2

Dear Jesus, Saint Nicholas was a wonderfully kind man.
He was always thinking of others and giving all he had.
Lord, please help us be generous like him.
Help us share what we have.
Help us see that the true gifts of this season
are love and generosity.
May we always share what we have
and give what we love.
We ask this through you, who guided Saint Nicholas,
one of our Christmas heroes. Amen.

DAY 3

Dear Father in heaven,
when Saint Lucy was a child
she was afraid of her mother's illness,
yet she never gave up hope.
Instead, she prayed constantly
for her mother to get well.
Thank you, Lord, for the gift of Saint Lucy.
Thank you for listening to us

no matter how big or small our prayers seem.
Thank you for being a father who welcomes us,
loves us, and keeps us close.
We thank you and praise you. Amen.

DAY 4

Dear Lord, Juan Diego was a simple farmer
devoted to faith in you.
You blessed him with a visit
from your mother, who honored him
with a miraculous picture
of her beautiful self on his *tilma*.
Even though life was hard for Juan Diego,
he always stayed close to you and your mother.
When times are hard,
especially during the Christmas season,
may they find the same hope in you.
May you and your mother wrap your arms around all of us,
who need your love this Christmas season
and all the days of the year. Amen.

DAY 5

Dear Lady of Guadalupe,
you appeared to Juan Diego and told him that
you listen to your children.
As our mother, you will love and protect us always.
We haven't a complaint, worry, or sadness
you won't listen to.
Our Lady, thank you for being such a good and kind mother.
Thank you for caring for us
as you did for your tiny baby, Jesus.
You protected him from the cold night,
and you protect us from all that harms us.
Thank you for loving us and keeping us safe always. Amen.

Incarnation

Was it hard or easy for Jesus to be both God and man?

PHILIPPIANS 2:5–11

Let the same mind be in you that was in Christ Jesus....[H]e humbled himself and became obedient to the point of death—even death on a cross. Therefore God also highly exalted him and gave him the name that is above every name, so that at the name of Jesus every knee should bend, in heaven and on earth and under the earth, and every tongue should confess that Jesus Christ is Lord, to the glory of God the Father.

DAY 1

Dear Jesus, you came to Earth to show us love.
Help us imitate you by being humble,
never thinking we're better than others.
Even though you were God,
you never held your power over others.
Instead, you served your brothers and sisters.
Please help us never control others
and remember that by loving others, we love you. Amen.

DAY 2

Dear heavenly Father,
thank you for sending us your son, Jesus.
Even though it's very hard for us
to understand the mystery of the incarnation,
it's not hard for us to know you loved us so much
that you sent your Son to Earth to show us how to love.
Help us never forget this mystery of our faith
and always give thanks for your great love. Amen.

DAY 3

Dear loving Jesus, you had a human soul, a human mind,
and a human will, yet you remained perfect.
Help us use our minds and our wills like you did.
Help us act like you so you will be fully formed inside us.
We ask this in the name of Jesus, who was perfect. Amen.

DAY 4

Dear Jesus, you showed what it is to be holy.
You strove for holiness.
Show us the path to holiness.
May we see every moment of every day
as an opportunity for us to be like you.
Stay with us in all we do and say. Amen.

DAY 5

Dear Jesus, you were human,
so you hurt and laughed and wept and felt just like we do.
When you were on Earth,
you felt everything we feel.
Because you knew temptation,
you make it easy for us to come to you when we fail.
Help us be the best friend to you that we possibly can. Amen.

The Immaculate Conception

When is it hard to say yes to God?

LUKE 1:46–50

And Mary said, "My soul magnifies the Lord, and my spirit rejoices in God my Savior, for he has looked with favor on the lowliness of his servant. Surely, from now on all generations will call me blessed; for the Mighty One has done great things for me, and holy is his name. His mercy is for those who fear him from generation to generation."

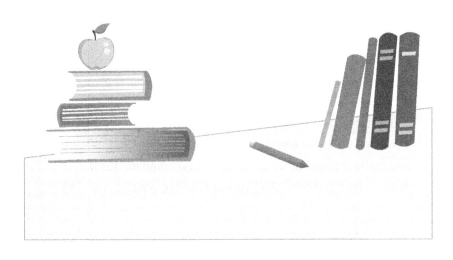

DAY 1

Lord, we thank you for the beautiful gift
of your mother, Mary, who was born without sin.
Her faith never wavered even during times of doubt.
Thank you for giving us your mother as an example
of how we should live our faith.
Help us model that same strength
to love you with our entire, heart, mind, soul, and body
so that someday we may all be together in heaven. Amen.

DAY 2

Dear Lord, what does it look like or feel like
to love with our entire heart?
Our mother, Mary, showed us that it means to
reach out with true compassion.
It means feeling others' pain when they're sad
and feeling their joy when they're happy.
Dear Lord, open our hearts so we always feel completely.
Fill our hearts with the same love
you and your mother have.
We ask this through Jesus,
whom Mary loved with all her heart. Amen.

DAY 3

Dear Lord, what is it like
to love with our entire mind?
When Mary watched the mean soldiers
whip you and make fun of you,
her heart was broken
yet she knew it was your will.
Help us strive to know
about you and your wonderful ways. Amen.

DAY 4

Dear Lord, what is it like
to love with our entire soul?
Our mother, Mary, showed us it means
saying yes to you in all we do.
Even when things are uncertain,
saying yes means putting our faith in you
just as Mary did when she said yes to the angel Gabriel.
Fill every corner of our souls with your spirit, Lord,
so that, like Mary, we may always be devoted to you. Amen.

DAY 5

Dear Lord, what is it like
to love with our entire body?
Like Mary, it means honoring you with all we do.
Lord, help us see our bodies as a gift.
Help us care for them wisely and with respect.
Help us to never use our body to hurt others.
May we always live so others can see
we are temples of your spirit.
We ask this through your mother,
whose body served you perfectly. Amen.

Christmas

What is the best gift you've ever given someone? Why?

LUKE 2:8–14

In that region there were shepherds living in the fields, keeping watch over their flock by night. Then an angel of the Lord stood before them, and the glory of the Lord shone around them, and they were terrified. But the angel said to them, "Do not be afraid; for see—I am bringing you good news of great joy for all the people: to you is born this day in the city of David a Saviour, who is the Messiah, the Lord. This will be a sign for you: you will find a child wrapped in bands of cloth and lying in a manger." And suddenly there was with the angel a multitude of the heavenly host, praising God and saying, "Glory to God in the highest heaven, and on earth peace among those whom he favors!"

DAY 1

All-giving Father, we thank you
for your baby son, Jesus.
On the day of his birth, heaven and Earth were joined in joy.
Help us always feel the joy of Jesus
and fill every day with his love,
his birth, his death, and his resurrection—
all eternal signs of his and your love for us.
We thank you in the name of
the choirs of angels who sing your praises. Amen.

DAY 2

Dear God, you sent your son, Jesus,
as the light of the world.
His birth broke through the darkness of sin
and brought hope and love to a world in desperate need.
Our world is still in need of his love and hope.
Continue to let the birth of Christ shine
as a beacon for those who live in darkness,
as hope for those who live in fear, and
as joy for those who live in sadness.
All things are possible through you. Amen.

DAY 3

Loving God, Christmas is a time of giving,
but sometimes we think it's more about receiving.
Fill us with your love this Christmas
so we remember that this day
isn't about toys or games or travel, but about *you*.
Help us realize that *Christ*
is the most important part of Christmas.
Bless us with the gift of giving.
Help us give your love, your peace,
and your joy all year. Amen.

DAY 4

Dear Jesus, everywhere we turn
we're persuaded to spend money.
Help us remember that money can't buy the best gifts.
Help us remember that loving words, loving actions,
loving thoughts, and loving gestures
are the true gifts of Christmas.
Help us remember that the gift of ourselves
is what this day is all about.
We ask this through you who gave yourself to us. Amen.

DAY 5

Dear God, the birthday of your son, Jesus,
was a day of eternal joy in heaven.
Thank you for our birthdays too.
When others celebrate our birthdays, we're reminded
we're an important part of your creation.
Help us respect ourselves as your special creations
and honor others on their special days.
Thank you for Christmas Day,
when we can celebrate Jesus' birth,
the most special birthday of all. Amen.

Giving and Receiving

*Would it be hard for you to give away
something you really like? Why?*

LUKE 21:1–4

*[Jesus] looked up and saw rich people putting their gifts into
the treasury; he also saw a poor widow put in two small copper coins. He said, "Truly I tell you, this poor widow has put in
more than all of them; for all of them have contributed out of
their abundance, but she out of her poverty has put in all she
had to live on."*

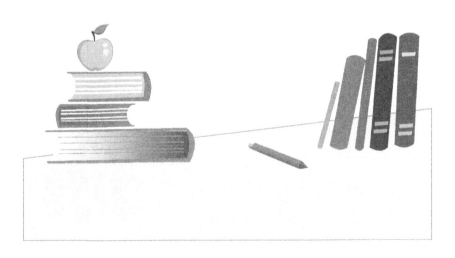

DAY 1

Dear God, you bless us every day
with all the things we need.
You even give us extra blessings.
Help us open our hearts
and our hands to give others what they need.
Help us be like you and think first of others
and what we can do for them.
If everyone shared, we would all have enough.
We ask this through you,
the giver of enough. Amen.

DAY 2

Dear heavenly God,
sometimes we're very greedy
and want more of everything.
May we see that more is not better.
May we see that more can hurt us.
May we see that more can be too much.
Lord, help us control our greed.
Help us see that it's enough
to have only what we need.
We ask this through Jesus, who taught us to live simply. Amen.

DAY 3

Dear holy Trinity—Father, Son, and Spirit—
through you, we see how we are called
to give and to live in relationships of love.
You help us see that people, not things, are important.
Fill us with your spirit of love
so we may always think of others first and ourselves last.
Help us understand that when we give,
we do it for them and not to make ourselves look good.
Our best gifts are unnoticed
by everyone except you. Amen.

DAY 4

Dear Jesus, sometimes it's hard to accept help
when we need it most.
Help us receive graciously.
Humble us, Lord, and
help us realize that sometimes everyone needs help.
Lord, help us see that
if we don't receive graciously,
others don't know the joy of giving.
We ask this through you, who accepted Simon's help
to carry your cross. Amen.

DAY 5

Dear Father, we know envy is a sin.
It makes us look at things others have
and wish we had them too.
It can even make us resentful or sad.
When we're jealous,
please fill our minds with your understanding
so we see the gifts we have
instead of the gifts we lack.
Fill our hearts with appreciation and
gratitude for good things.
Most of all, help us praise and honor you
for the wonderful gift of your son, Jesus. Amen.

Epiphany

What brings you closer to Jesus?

ADAPTED FROM MATTHEW 2:1–12

In the time of King Herod, after Jesus was born in Bethlehem wise men from the East came to Jerusalem asking, "Where is this child who has been born king of the Jews? For we observed his star at its rising and have come to pay him homage." When King Herod heard this, he was frightened. And... he asked where the Messiah was born. They told him in Bethlehem. Then Herod called the three wise men and sent them on to Bethlehem, saying, "Return and tell me where this King is."...And they followed the star until it stopped, and they were filled with joy. On entering, they found Mary and the child Jesus and knelt down and presented him with the gifts of gold, frankincense, and myrrh. And having been warned in a dream not to return to Herod, they went home by another road.

DAY 1

Dear Jesus, you are our true gift on this Epiphany.
We celebrate you who give yourself to us freely and perfectly.
Thank you for being our shining star and leading us
to a way of holiness and humility.
As your angels protected you from King Herod,
may they protect us from evil.
May your angels and your love surround us.
May the star of Bethlehem always shine,
leading us to you. We pray. Amen.

DAY 2

Dear Jesus, you weren't like other kings.
Most kings live in a palace and have jewels
and crowns and royal clothes and servants.
You were born in a stable and lived a simple life.
You are a king who serves others.
Please help us be like you.
Help us always serve you and your Father.
Teach us to love your kingdom and its children just as you do.
We ask this through you who
built your kingdom on Earth. Amen.

DAY 3

Dear Jesus, the wise men followed a star in the sky.
It led them to Bethlehem and to you.
Sometimes we follow the wrong things,
and instead of getting closer to you,
we get further from you.
Help us always stay focused on you,
just like the wise men were.
Never allow us to put things in front of us
that will keep our eyes off you.
You are our shining star.
Shine for us so the path to you is always lit. Amen.

DAY 4

Dear Jesus, the three kings brought you gold,
one of the most precious metals.
Through the gift of gold,
help us see that all that you created is precious.
Help us see that our classmates, our families,
our lives, and our world
are your precious creations.
Fill us with love and thanksgiving
for the most precious gift of all,
your Body and Blood
through the gift of the Eucharist. Amen.

DAY 5

Dear Jesus, the three kings brought you
frankincense and myrrh.
One reminds us of the importance of our bodies,
and the other reminds us of the importance of
lifting up our prayers and thoughts to you.
Just as myrrh anoints a body,
help us anoint others' lives.
May frankincense help us remember
that everything we do rises up to you.
Let every action we make be a prayer.
We ask this through you,
who honored everyone you met
and who taught us to pray. Amen.

Holy Family

When is it hard to be part of a family?

COLOSSIANS 3:12–16

As God's chosen ones, holy and beloved, clothe yourselves with compassion, kindness, humility, meekness, and patience. Bear with one another and, if anyone has a complaint against another, forgive each other; just as the Lord has forgiven you, so you also must forgive. Above all, clothe yourselves with love, which binds everything together in perfect harmony.

DAY 1

Dear good and gracious God,
we gather today in thanksgiving for family.
Families come in all shapes and sizes.
Families help us learn about you!
Help us see the beauty of our families
and appreciate all they do for us.
Help us see that they love us for who we are.
Most important, thank you for welcoming us into your family
and for letting us be called children of God. Amen.

DAY 2

Dear Jesus, you were part of the Holy Family
and lived a life of holiness.
Help us see that our families are holy too.
Fill our hearts with the same love
you had for your parents
so we may act in a loving way to our moms and dads.
Dear Jesus, stay with us always
so that someday we may join
your Holy Family in heaven. Amen.

DAY 3

Dear Jesus, you were a child, so you know
how difficult it is sometimes to be part of a family.
When we're tempted to disobey our parents,
help us be strong.
When we want to be left alone,
help us see that families are about togetherness.
When we look at other families and wish they were ours,
help us see the uniqueness of our own families.
Help all families who struggle to love one another. Amen.

DAY 4

Dear Holy Family, how blessed we are to have you
as a model of what a family should be.
Your family knew sadness and joy and fear,
yet never wavered in faith.
Help our families live in peace and not let pride
or selfishness or self-importance cause pain.
Guide our families to stay rooted in love. Amen.

DAY 5

Dear Holy Trinity, thank you for the gift of our parents,
who brought us to you for the gift of baptism.
Open our eyes to see that through our baptism
we are part of a larger family—your family on Earth.
Fill our hearts with your love
so we will love and care for all your children
as our brothers and sisters in Christ.
May we see their needs to be as important as ours.
We ask this through our brother, Jesus,
who showed us what love for you really looks like. Amen.

Mission

WEEK 24

Christian Unity

How has Jesus' message of love and hope changed the world?

LUKE 9:18–20

Once when Jesus was praying alone, with only the disciples near him, he asked them, "Who do the crowds say that I am?" They answered, "John the Baptist; but others, Elijah; and still others, that one of the ancient prophets has arisen." He said to them, "But who do you say that I am?" Peter answered, "The Messiah of God."

DAY 1

Dear Jesus, thank you for coming to Earth
to show us a new way to live.
Thank you for giving the apostles the courage
to spread the Good News.
We're happy that we and our school
can be counted among your believers. Amen.

DAY 2

Dear Jesus, you worked hard
to teach the apostles who you are.
Before you left, you commanded them
to go forth and teach all nations.
Jesus, give us the strength and courage to be your disciples.
Fill us with your Spirit so we can go forth
and, by our actions, show the world your message
of love for all. Amen.

DAY 3

Dear Jesus, how proud you must be
that so many believers follow you.
Please unite Christian communities throughout the world.
Help us see that in spite of our different paths to you,
we are *all* believers in you.
We celebrate our differences and our common beliefs.
Fill us with your Spirit
so the world will know we're Christians
by our love for you and for one another. Amen.

DAY 4

Dear Jesus, forgive us when we don't defend our faith.
Forgive us for the times we would rather be about
our interests rather than yours.
When we fail, give us the strength of the apostles to get up
and keep going forward, one step at a time.
Thank you for never giving up on us. Amen.

DAY 5

Dear heavenly Father, how proud
you must be of your son, Jesus.
Please help all believers
to continue his way of living.
Help us grow in love for you and for one another.
Open our eyes to see that we are *all* your followers.
Unite us so that together we can
create your kingdom on Earth. Amen.

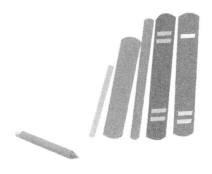

World Peace

*Have you ever felt the peace of Jesus
within you? When?*

ADAPTED FROM JOHN 14:25–27

*[Jesus said,] "I have said these things to you while I am still
with you. But the Advocate, the Holy Spirit, whom the Father
will send in my name, will teach you everything, and remind
you of all that I have said to you. Peace I leave with you; my
peace I give to you. I do not give to you as the world gives.
Do not let your hearts be troubled, and do not let them be
afraid."*

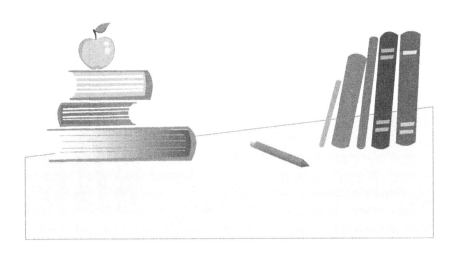

DAY 1

Dear Jesus, how wonderful you are
to fill us with your peace.
Sometimes it seems like we could never
make a difference,
but you showed us it's possible.
By your good works, we see that one person
can make a difference.
We know that if we truly live as peaceful people,
we can make a difference.
Help us be all we can be.
Help us be the instruments of peace you call us to be.
We ask this through you,
the never-ending source of peace and love. Amen.

DAY 2

Dear Jesus, we are your followers.
Help us work for peace among all your people.
Help us see that color, race, creed,
and gender aren't reasons to exclude others.
As your true followers, we know that if we want peace,
we must also work for justice.
We must work for a world where everything is fair,
where everyone has what he or she needs to live.
Help us, Lord, to make this world a place where
children everywhere can be happy.
We ask this through you, who said,
"Let the little children come to me." Amen.

DAY 3

Dear Jesus, when there is conflict, peace is absent.
We've all been part of conflict.
Forgive us for bringing trouble
to our families, our classrooms, and our friendships.
Guide us to be calm or walk away when troubles arise.

Help us not say mean things or accuse others.
Help us not judge others or hold grudges.
Fill us with the gift of peacemaking so we can learn
to be your peace on Earth. Amen.

DAY 4

Dear Jesus, violence is everywhere.
This must make you very sad,
because you hated violence.
You taught everyone to treat others gently
and with respect and kindness.
Lord, we know all things are possible through you.
Help make this world peaceful.
Open the eyes of world leaders to see that
violence and war are not the only ways to peace.
Guide them and us so we may be people
of peace and love and not of violence and hate.
We ask this through you who can do all things. Amen.

DAY 5

Dear heavenly creator, all life is precious.
Open our hearts to see
that we must honor every form of life.
When we honor life, we honor *you*.
When we protect every form of life,
we protect your creation.
When we celebrate every form of life,
we celebrate the wonder of you.
Lord, if we lived in wonder of each other,
peace would follow.
We make this our prayer to you,
our God of wonder and might. Amen.

Diversity

*How do you show respect for people
you don't know?*

GENESIS 1:27–28

*So God created humankind in his image, in the image of God
he created them; male and female he created them. God
blessed them, and God said to them, "Be fruitful and multiply,
and fill the earth and subdue it; and have dominion over the
fish of the sea and over the birds of the air and over every living thing that moves upon the earth."*

DAY 1

Dear God, we can only imagine how big you are
by looking at the world you created.
You are present in each of us beyond every race and culture.
Help us appreciate you and all you have created.
Help us see your presence in each of us
and in every race, color, and size.
Each of our talents is also present in you!
No wonder you're so *awesome* and can do all things.
Thank you for the gift of our diversity
and for calling us each your children. Amen.

DAY 2

Dear heavenly creator, *diverse* means different.
Sometimes we think of different as bad.
Sometimes we're afraid of others who don't look like us.
Please forgive us and fill us with your spirit of wisdom
to help us see that different is good.
If everything looked the same,
think how boring our lives would be.
You made us different to make life interesting and fun.
Thank you for giving us what is best for us. Amen.

DAY 3

Dear Holy Trinity—Father, Son, and Spirit—
through you, we see that we are called
to live together in harmony.
Thank you, Father, for creating
each of us in a unique way.
Brother Jesus, thank you for teaching us
to love one another.
Holy Spirit, thank you for filling us
with your spirit of compassion so we can
learn to live together in peace.
May we always give you glory and praise. Amen.

DAY 4

Dear Jesus, you never treated anyone with disrespect.
Even though you were made fun of because of your friends,
you never turned back.
Sometimes we judge others by what they wear,
how they look, and what they do.
Help us stop doing that. Help us be a friend to all
and find the good—*you*!—in everyone.
May others not judge us
but treat us with the same love you do.
We ask this through you who love us best of all. Amen.

Dear Father, so many times we're not happy
with ourselves and how we look.
Help us see that you love
the way we look and the way we are.
Help us never wish we could be like someone else.
Help us love one another and ourselves the same way.
Thank for being you—exactly as you are. Amen.

WEEK 27

Social Justice

*Have you ever spoken up for someone who
needed your help?*

ISAIAH 58:6–7, 9B–10

*Is not this the fast that I choose: to loose the bonds of injustice,
to undo the thongs of the yoke, to let the oppressed go free,
and to break every yoke? Is it not to share your bread with the
hungry, and bring the homeless poor into your house; when
you see the naked, to cover them, and not to hide yourself
from your own kin?...If you remove the yoke from among you,
the pointing of the finger, the speaking of evil, if you offer
your food to the hungry and satisfy the needs of the afflicted,
then your light shall rise in the darkness.*

DAY 1

Lord, we give thanks that we belong to a Church
that cares about everyone.
Help us learn with our minds
and our hearts what is right and good
and what we can do to carry out this mission of our Church.
Help us be aware of others' needs.
Help us be like the prophet Isaiah by reminding others
that we must care for your world.
We ask this through Jesus, who cares for us all. Amen.

DAY 2

Dear Lord, from the beginning of creation
you dreamed of a world in harmony.
We can help your dream become real
by sharing all you have created.
Humans, just like plants and animals, need care to grow.
Help us always care for and respect all life.
Help us realize that everything
you've created is sacred.
Help us treat everyone with dignity,
especially teachers and classmates.
May we always make you proud of us
as we take care of your world. Amen.

DAY 3

Dear Lord, you dream of a world where
we all have the things we need to live—
housing, food, clothing, and education.
Help us fight for a world
where we all have what we need.
Thank you for all we have.
Help us share what we don't need
with those who have less than us.
Help us never be selfish with what we have

and with what we can give.
Comfort people whose lives are difficult
because they don't have what they need.
We ask this in the name of your Son,
who offers comfort and love to all. Amen.

Dear Lord, thank you for jobs and for the ability to work.
Help us always respect workers.
Through our work, we share in your plan
for a world that lives in harmony.
Work changes our world and us.
When we work hard, we feel good.
Help us respect the workers in our school
and to always be cheerful and appreciate what they do.
Help us do the best we can
at any job we undertake.
We ask this through Jesus,
who worked miracles for those he loved. Amen.

Dear Lord, we're part of your human family.
Forgive us when we forget that.
Families care for one another, protect one another,
speak for one another, encourage one another,
and respect one another.
Fill us with your compassion
so that when our brothers and sister
across the world are in need,
we help them, share their pain or suffering,
and pray that your spirit
of generous abundance will move upon them.
We ask this through your Son,
who met the needs of all. Amen.

Catholic Schools Week

*What makes your school different
from other schools?*

MATTHEW 28:16–20

*Now the eleven disciples went to Galilee, to the mountain
to which Jesus had directed them. When they saw him, they
worshipped him; but some doubted. And Jesus came and said
to them, "All authority in heaven and on earth has been given
to me. Go therefore and make disciples of all nations, baptizing them in the name of the Father and of the Son and of the
Holy Spirit, and teaching them to obey everything that I have
commanded you. And remember, I am with you always, to the
end of the age."*

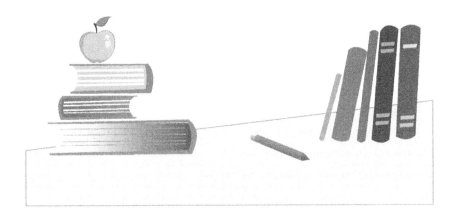

DAY 1

Dear God, thank you for the gift of our Catholic faith.
Help us always treasure it as a way
to be closer to you.
Thank you for the opportunity to learn in a Catholic school.
Help our school be a place of learning with our hearts
as well as our minds.
Guide us on our Catholic journey of education.
Through your guidance,
we can enter our school to learn about you
and go forth from school each day to serve you and one another. Amen.

DAY 2

Dear Jesus, education is not available to all boys and girls.
Help us always appreciate education as a special gift.
Bless the teachers, administrators, parents,
and community who make our Catholic education possible.
Help us make this a just world
where everyone's needs are met,
so that all children will have both access to you
and knowledge of your world.
We ask this through your son, Jesus,
who reigns with justice. Amen.

DAY 3

Dear Father in heaven, *catholic* means we welcome all and
spread the Good News to the corners of the Earth.
Help us, Lord, to make our classrooms centers of care
where we set a good example for others
and our actions glorify you.
We ask this through Jesus,
whose death and resurrection glorified each of us. Amen.

DAY 4

Dear God, thank you for the sacraments, the seven special ways
Catholics get closer to you and live in your grace.
Thank you for initiating us into your faith
through baptism, the Eucharist, and confirmation.
Thank you for the sacrament of healing, which
comforts us when we're vulnerable,
and thank you for filling us with your love
as we journey through our vocations.
May we always be sacramental people who reflect you
and your attitudes to the world around us. Amen.

DAY 5

Dear Father, you filled our heads with the ability to think,
to feel, and to find our way to you.
Thank you for the gift of judgment,
which allows us to make choices.
Being Catholic means involving our hearts in our choices.
May our Catholic education
teach us to make good decisions
that affect others and the world.
Help us learn well, speak out for a just world,
and value all life as a blessing.
Most of all, we thank you for coming
into our classrooms every day. Amen.

Trinity

Which person of the Trinity do you pray to most? Why?

MATTHEW 28:16–20

Now the eleven disciples went to Galilee, to the mountain to which Jesus had directed them. When they saw him, they worshipped him; but some doubted. And Jesus came and said to them, "All authority in heaven and on earth has been given to me. Go therefore and make disciples of all nations, baptizing them in the name of the Father and of the Son and of the Holy Spirit, and teaching them to obey everything that I have commanded you. And remember, I am with you always, to the end of the age."

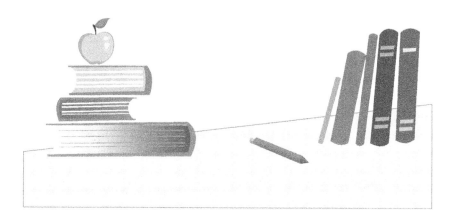

DAY 1

Holy Trinity, we honor and praise you as
our creator, our savior, and our sanctifier.
Fill us with your love so
we can enter fully into your mystery.
Strengthen our faith so we can always believe in you.
May we be living examples of your love.
We ask this through you,
the Father, the Son, and the Holy Spirit,
forever and ever. Amen.

DAY 2

Dear God, you created heaven and Earth,
and your love for us
is constantly evident in the ongoing revelation of creation.
Thank you for the beautiful gift of our world.
Help us take good care of it
and value each form of life.
Open our eyes to the beauty
and uniqueness of every living thing.
May we always know our world
is the reflection of your love for us.
We ask this through your son, Jesus,
who taught us to honor you. Amen.

DAY 3

Dear Jesus, you who are both God and Man
came to Earth to teach us to love.
May we learn from your courage to never give up,
even when things are hard.
May we learn from your friendship that
everyone we meet is our brother or sister.
May we learn from your compassion
that we must never judge others.

May we learn from your love
that we are called to love others.
Help us live every day as you did,
giving glory to God. Amen.

DAY 4

Holy Spirit, you are present in us and in our world.
May we always feel you
guiding and strengthening us.
When we are discouraged, breathe new life in us.
When we are unsure, fill us with your spirit of peace.
When we are discouraged, carry us on your wings.
When we are joyous, may we sing your praises.
Thank you for your never-ending presence,
now and forever. Amen.

DAY 5

Blessed Father, Son, and Holy Spirit—three-in-one—
you teach us that relationships of love
are key to our faith in you and in one another.
Help us respect others.
Help us uphold the dignity of those we love.
When we struggle in our relationships,
give us the courage to persevere.
By seeing your presence in everyone,
we are called to your holiness.
Thank you for your eternal love and care for us. Amen.

Service

What do you like about serving someone?

JAMES 2:1–4, 14

If a person with gold rings and in fine clothes comes into your assembly, and if a poor person in dirty clothes also comes in, and if you take notice of the one wearing the fine clothes and say, 'Have a seat here, please', while to the one who is poor you say, 'Stand there', or, 'Sit at my feet', have you not made distinctions among yourselves, and become judges with evil thoughts?...What good is it...if you say you have faith but do not have works?

DAY 1

Lord Jesus, you taught us how to serve.
On the night before you died,
you washed your apostles' feet to remind us
that even if we're asked to do something unpleasant,
we must do it lovingly because we're called to help others.
Thank you for serving us every moment. Amen.

DAY 2

Dear Jesus, help us be like you.
Help us see the many talents you've given us,
and help us use them to serve others.
Thank you for teaching us that talents are not to be buried,
but to be shared with others.
Help us encourage, support, give, comfort, speak,
embrace, listen, share, and be present to one another. Amen.

DAY 3

Loving God, sometimes we think of ourselves before others.
Forgive us, Lord, when we haven't done what we could have,
when we don't help around the house,
when we're too lazy to clean our rooms,
when we roll our eyes when asked to help a classmate.
Help us see that every time we serve,
we're serving you. Amen.

DAY 4

Dear Lord, you taught us that greatness
isn't about being popular or athletic or
about winning prizes or awards.
You taught us that greatness is about serving others.
Greatness is about deeds, not things.
Help us do good deeds so that one day
we'll be counted as one of your heroes. Amen.

DAY 5

Dear Lord, be with us as we support our families,
our schools, our communities, and our world.
Thank you for showing us that when we help others,
we receive much more than we gave.
Thank you for showing us that even the littlest things
can make a difference. Amen.

Section 6

Morality

WEEK 31

The Ten Commandments

*Do the Ten Commandments
make life easier or harder?*

EXODUS 20:1-2, 7–8, 12–17

I am the LORD your God, who brought you out of the land of Egypt, out of the house of slavery; you shall have no other gods before me.....You shall not make wrongful use of the name of the LORD your God....Remember the sabbath day, and keep it holy. Honor your father and your mother, so that your days may be long in the land that the LORD your God is giving you. You shall not murder. You shall not commit adultery. You shall not steal. You shall not bear false witness against your neighbor. You shall not covet...anything that belongs to your neighbor.

DAY 1

Heavenly Father, you gave your people
the Ten Commandments to help them follow you.
Send your Holy Spirit
to help us act in ways that will please you
and help us follow your commandments.
May we always put you first,
and may we live every day mindful of our neighbors' needs.
We ask this through the communion of saints,
whose lives show us how to be your true followers. Amen.

DAY 2

Heavenly Father, how sad you must be
when we fall away from your laws
and fail to give you the honor and respect you deserve.
We're sorry for thinking about things
instead of about you and your blessings.
We're sorry for using bad language
and for using your name in anger.
We're sorry for the times we haven't gone to Mass
because we were tired or lazy
or because we wanted to do something else.
Forgive us for these failings. Help us honor you always. Amen.

DAY 3

Dear Creator God, thank you for our parents.
How blessed we are to have you, our heavenly Father,
and earthly parents to guide and protect us.
May we always give our parents
the honor and respect they deserve.
Help us understand that just because
we disagree with them doesn't mean
they're not acting in our best interest.
Help us be the best children we can be
so someday we can all be happy in heaven together. Amen.

DAY 4

Dear Lord, it's easy for us to forget
that when we're unkind to others,
when we take things that do not belong to us,
when we do not tell the truth,
or when we withhold our friendship,
we're doing that to you as well.
Help us treat others with kindness,
to respect them and their possessions,
and to never be jealous.
Fill us with your love
so we can share in their joy.
We ask this through Jesus, who always put others first. Amen.

DAY 5

Dear God, thank you for creating us
in your image and likeness
and for filling us with your spirit.
Teach us to love one another and ourselves.
Help us respect our bodies as part of you
and as little churches of your holiness.
May we never do anything to disrespect our bodies
or others' bodies,
but to always strive to use them
to glorify and praise you as our loving Father. Amen.

The Beatitudes

Why do you think Jesus gave us the beatitudes?

MATTHEW 5:1–12

When Jesus saw the crowds, he went up the mountain; and after he sat down, his disciples came to him. Then he began to speak, and taught them, saying:

"Blessed are the poor in spirit, for theirs is the kingdom of heaven.

"Blessed are those who mourn, for they will be comforted.

"Blessed are the meek, for they will inherit the earth.

"Blessed are those who hunger and thirst for righteousness, for they will be filled.

"Blessed are the merciful, for they will receive mercy.

"Blessed are the pure in heart, for they will see God.

"Blessed are the peacemakers, for they will be called children of God.

"Blessed are those who are persecuted for righteousness' sake, for theirs is the kingdom of heaven.

"Blessed are you when people revile you and persecute you and utter all kinds of evil against you falsely on my account. Rejoice and be glad, for your reward is great in heaven, for in the same way they persecuted the prophets who were before you."

DAY 1

Heavenly Father, thank you for sending your son,
Jesus, to teach us how to live.
Through our baptism, we became members of your kingdom,
and we are called to live by your ways.
Help us have attitudes of kindness
and compassion toward our neighbors.
Fill us with the happiness that caring for others brings.
Help us always be grateful for your Son,
and help us live more like him. Amen.

DAY 2

Dear Jesus, you taught us to be pure in spirit,
to feel sorry for others, and to be humble.
Please help us never make our *things*
more important to us than *you.*
When we see sad people, help us share their pain.
By living out your ways,
we can someday be happy with you in heaven. Amen.

DAY 3

Dear Jesus, the beatitudes teach us to live with justice,
to have mercy for others, and to be pure in spirit.
Help us always fight for fairness for everyone, not just for us.
We can show mercy by forgiving others
just as you forgive us for our failings.
And when we live a life centered in your teachings,
we can be pure in spirit.
Please give us what we need to be your true disciples
and to carry out your dream of a just world for all. Amen.

DAY 4

Dear Jesus, it's sometimes hard to follow your beatitudes.
People may make fun of us
when we try to do what is right.
Help us always live in peace.
When others get crabby or angry,
help us smooth things out.
If someone is angry, help us remain calm.
You tell us that when we're peacemakers,
we can be called your child.
Nothing makes us happier
than to make you proud and to be yours! Amen.

DAY 5

Dear Jesus, living with new attitudes
that teach us how to *be* your true disciples is exciting.
It's also difficult, because everyone doesn't live your way.
Send your Holy Spirit
so we can live as your true followers.
Fill this world with your loving spirit so that someday
we can live in a just world
where all people have what they need.
We ask this through you who are all-loving. Amen.

Forgiveness

When was it hard for you to forgive? Why?

MATTHEW 18:21–22

Then Peter came and said to him, "Lord, if another member of the church sins against me, how often should I forgive? As many as seven times?" Jesus said to him, "Not seven times, but, I tell you, seventy-seven times."

DAY 1

Merciful God, we thank you for always forgiving us.
You tell us that nothing we do
will make you love us less.
Thank you for unconditional love.
Thank you for always being there to cheer us on.
Help us be strong like Jesus.
When temptation comes our way,
help us turn away from sin
and turn to you, our all-loving, all-forgiving Father. Amen.

Dear Jesus, when Peter asked you how many time we should
forgive, you told him *seventy-seven* times.
That was your way of saying we should *always* forgive others.
Thank you for teaching us that even though others hurt us;
by forgiving them we can let go of our anger and resentment.
Your healing power can mend the hurt that is often left behind.
Please strengthen us and give us a forgiving heart like yours.
Amen.

DAY 3

Dear Jesus, forgiveness feels good!
It fills us with your grace and makes us more like you.
Because we have been hurt, it is sometimes hard to forgive.
We do things we're ashamed of,
and it's hard to forgive ourselves.
Help us see that we're still your children.
You love us unconditionally. If *you* can forgive us,
we should certainly forgive ourselves.
Help us learn from our mistakes. Amen.

DAY 4

Dear kind and forgiving Jesus,
you gave the apostles the power to forgive sins.
This was the first reconciliation.
Thank you for the sacrament of reconciliation.
Thank you for letting us come to you
in sorrow and love and be forgiven
for *every* sin we've committed.
Thank you for the saving grace
you give us through absolution.
Finally, Lord, thank you for always
allowing us to start over. Amen.

DAY 5

Gentle and compassionate Jesus,
when you were dying on the cross,
you forgave those who crucified you.
You put your own suffering aside
and reached out to others.
Forgive us for the times we were selfish and uncaring.
Forgive us for the times we hurt others.
Thank you for knowing our strengths and weaknesses
and for loving us just as we are.
You always believe in us.
Help us always believe in you.
For this, we pray. Amen.

Decision-Making

Think of a time when you made a poor decision. What should you have done differently? Why?

MATTHEW 4:1–11

Then Jesus was led up by the Spirit into the wilderness to be tempted by the devil. He fasted for forty days and forty nights, and afterwards he was famished....The devil took him to a very high mountain and showed him all the kingdoms of the world and their splendor; and he said to him, "All these I will give you, if you will fall down and worship me." Jesus said to him, "Away with you, Satan! for it is written, 'Worship the Lord your God, and serve only him.'"

DAY 1

Dear Jesus, sometimes it's easier to do the wrong thing.
Help us when we're too lazy to help someone,
or when it's easier to steal someone else's answer.
Fill us with your Spirit to help us make wise decisions.
Keep us always looking at you and your ways.
We ask this through you, who taught us to say *no*. Amen.

DAY 2

Dear Jesus, it takes courage to make good decisions.
Sometimes we're afraid to do the right thing
because others will make fun of us.
Give us the courage to stand up for
someone who is being bullied.
We know you can help us with every decision
as long as we ask for help.
Thank you for always being there. Amen.

DAY 3

Dear God, sometimes we show off and
brag about what we've done.
With your help, we can turn away
from our selfishness and turn to you
who are deserving of our love and attention.
Please never give up on us,
even when we disappoint you. Amen.

DAY 4

Dear Jesus, bad habits are hard to break.
When we make bad choices over and over again,
help us see that we are turning away from you and your ways.
Stay with us as we struggle to make the right decision,
and rejoice with us when we return to your ways.
We ask this through Jesus,
who fought the battle of good over evil for us. Amen.

DAY 5

Dear Jesus, you taught us that through prayer,
 all things are possible.
When we have a tough decision to make, help us stop and pray.
When we falter, give us the wisdom
to think of what you would want us to do.
Thank you for your gift of the Holy Spirit. Amen.

Lent

WEEK 35

Ash Wednesday

*What needs changing in
your relationship with God?*

JOEL 2:12–13

*Yet even now, says the LORD, return to me with all your heart,
with fasting, with weeping, and with mourning; rend your
hearts and not your clothing. Return to the LORD, your God,
for he is gracious and merciful, slow to anger, and abounding
in steadfast love.*

DAY 1

Dear Jesus, on Ash Wednesday,
ashes remind us that we are a small part of God's creation.
They remind us that we're no better than anyone,
and they humble us before you and others.
Help us see that you love each of us exactly the same. Amen.

DAY 2

Dear Jesus, Lent is forty days long to help us remember
the forty days you spent in the desert.
Satan tempted you with food, power, and glory,
but you said, "Away with you, Satan!"
Help us say no just like you did.
After forty days, may we be the best "we" we can be! Amen.

DAY 3

Dear Jesus, when you fasted in the desert,
you must have been very hungry.
During this Lenten season, help us fast.
Help us realize that some boys and girls are *always* hungry.
Maybe by giving up our favorite food or drink or candy,
We can have an idea of how that feels.
Give us the strength to do this and help us offer up
this sacrifice to you who sacrificed yourself for us. Amen.

DAY 4

Dear Jesus, during Lent we are asked to give alms.
That means sharing what we have with others.
Many children don't have what they need.
They don't have warm clothes.
This Lenten season, help us think about others.
Help us look at the things we have,
figure out what we no longer need,
and then share what we can spare. Amen.

DAY 5

Dear God, prayer is the way we talk to you.
Like any *awesome* parent, you love it when we talk to you.
Forgive us when we forget to pray.
Help us talk to you *every* day.
Help us always thank you for our blessings,
praise you for your goodness, and ask you for forgiveness.

Fill us with your Spirit, Lord, so we will listen
and hear you when you speak.
We ask this through your son, Jesus, who taught us to pray.
Amen.

WEEK 36

Conversion

*Have you ever asked God to help you change
the way you do something?*

ADAPTED FROM LUKE 19:1–10

Jesus was passing through the town of Jericho. A man named Zacchaeus was very rich because he had cheated people out of money. He climbed a tree so he could see Jesus through the crowds. When Jesus saw him, he said, "Zacchaeus, come down, I am going to your house today." The people were mad that Jesus would go to the house of a sinner. Zacchaeus said to Jesus, "Lord, I will change my ways and I will give half my money to the poor and pay back four times what I have cheated others out of." And Jesus forgave him.

DAY 1

Dear Jesus, by visiting Zacchaeus' house,
you showed us you love us just the way we are.
You don't favor those who are popular or rich or smart.
When you enter our hearts,
we begin to change through love.
Our hard hearts soften and become more like yours.
Help us, Lord, to be like Zacchaeus,
to welcome you into our hearts
so we can change our sinful ways
and become more like you. Amen.

DAY 2

Forgiving Father, sometimes we don't know
the power of our sinful ways
until we look behind us and
see the damage we've done.
Lord, help us not always look forward.
Help us also look back and look sideways
so we can get a clear view
of how our actions will affect others.
Change our hearts so we don't do only
what is best for us, but also
what is best for those around us.
We ask this through Jesus,
who always thought about others first. Amen.

DAY 3

Dear Jesus, most of the time we think *we're* in control.
Then something happens, and we realize *you* are.
Help us when we feel out of control.
Help us see that we need to change our thinking—
let go and let you be in charge.
Then, no matter what happens, you are with us.

You light the way for us.
We ask this through you,
the light of the world. Amen.

DAY 4

Dear Jesus, when you are the source of our goodness,
we will always follow your ways.
Sometimes when we think no one is watching,
it's easy to do the wrong thing.
We forget you can see everything we do
and all of the consequences.
Watch over us, Lord, so we're always honest.
Guide us to always do the right thing
so others will know we're
trustworthy, dependable, honest, and true.
We ask this through you,
whom we can always depend on. Amen.

DAY 5

Dear Jesus, you were human, so you know
what it's like to be tempted.
Sometimes peer pressure, TV, and movies
convince us to make bad decisions.
Forgive us when we use your gifts
in ways that hurt us or others.
Turn our hearts to focus on you
and do what you expect us to.
When we're committed to you,
we grow in faith and love
and in hope of being with you forever. Amen.

Perseverance

Have you ever finished something even though it was hard to finish? How did you feel?

ADAPTED FROM LUKE 11:5–13

And Jesus said to them, "Suppose you have a friend, and you go to him at midnight and say to him, 'Friend, lend me three loaves of bread.' And he answers from within, 'Do not bother me. The door has already been locked and my children are already in bed.' But you keep on asking for bread. Eventually he will get up and give you what you need because of your perseverance. In the same way, I say to you, ask and it will be given to you; search and you will find; knock and the door will be opened to you."

DAY 1

Ever-loving God, Jesus taught us to
never stop praying for what we want.
Help us see that sometimes what we want isn't what we need.
When we think you don't seem to hear our prayers,
help us remember that you know what is best for us.
Open our hearts to hear and accept
all the answers to our prayers.
In thanks, we pray. Amen.

DAY 2

Dear Jesus, when we set goals,
we keep our eyes focused
on what is important to us.
Our main goal is to be happy with you in heaven.
Help us stay focused on you
and never stray from that goal.
Help us persevere in pursuing our goals
so that by using our gifts,
we can fulfill your dreams.
We ask this through you, who accomplished
your goal of defeating sin. Amen.

DAY 3

Dear Holy Spirit, through you
we receive the gift of perseverance
to help us withstand
anything that comes our way.
We want to be good at things right away,
but we know that isn't always possible.
Things that are important, like skills and achievements,
take time and practice.
Lord, give us the patience and perseverance
to hang in there even when it seems to take forever
to accomplish or achieve something.
Help us persevere. When we do,
we are the best we can be. Amen.

DAY 4

Heavenly Father, when you carried your cross to Calvary,
it would have been easy to drop it and say,
"I don't want to do this."
Instead, you kept going.
You persevered for *us*!
Thank you, dear Jesus, for dying on the cross for our sins.
Because you persevered, you won heaven for us.
When things get hard, help us pick up our cross
as you did yours.
Help us persevere so we can be happy with you in heaven.
Amen.

DAY 5

Dear God, coaches cheer us on and encourage us to do our best.
Thank you for being our most important coach
and never giving up on us,
even when we turn our backs on you.
Thank you for forgiving us when we don't try our best.
Thank you for all the people who cheer us on:
parents, siblings, teachers, friends.
Help us be a coach.
When we see someone struggling,
help us find the right words of encouragement
to overcome any battle.
We ask this through your son, Jesus,
our biggest fan. Amen.

Obedience

What would happen if there were no laws?

DEUTERONOMY 28:1–2

If you will only obey the LORD your God, by diligently observing all his commandments that I am commanding you today, the LORD your God will set you high above all the nations of the earth; all these blessings shall come upon you and overtake you, if you obey the LORD your God.

DAY 1

Dear heavenly Father, you gave us
the Ten Commandments to keep order
and to help us grow in love for you and for one another.
Laws help keep order in our world.
Thank you for loving us so much
that you gave us boundaries
and commandments that show us
how to love you and our neighbor.
Please help us honor your commandments
and do what you ask.
We ask this through your son, Jesus,
who obeyed you in all ways. Amen.

DAY 2

Dear Jesus, you died on the cross for us
because your Father asked you to.
What a tough job.
You put your life in God's hands
and trusted that he knew what was best for everyone.
You showed us what it means to obey.
Lord, when we don't want to obey our parents,
teachers, or those in authority, help us be like you.
Help us understand that they are doing what is best.
Thank you for being beside us always. Amen.

DAY 3

Dear Father above, being in power can be fun.
We can make rules, boss others around,
and make people do what we want them to do.
But that isn't always right.
When we use our power well,
we make rules and ask others to do things
that are good for them, not us.
That's the kind of powerful God you are.
You never think of yourself.
You always put our needs first.
Help us do the same.
May we always be good leaders modeled on you. Amen.

DAY 4

Dear mother Mary, you obeyed God
even though you were uncertain about what was ahead.
You didn't cry, *"Why me, God?"*
You said, "Let it be with me according to your word."
Sometimes we're like that.
But sometimes our parents ask us to do something,
and we ask, "Why?"
When they answer, "Because I said so,"
we become frustrated.
Help us understand what they are really saying is,
"You may not understand right now,
but trust that I know what is best for you."
Guide us, mother Mary, so we may always
trust our parents' love just as you did. Amen.

DAY 5

Dear God, it's hard to obey,
especially when it seems like
everyone can make rules except us.
What would it be like without rules?
If everyone did whatever they wanted,
the world would be a scary place.
You taught us the Laws of Love to help us do our best.
Rules at home help us play safely, get rest, and live neatly.
Rules in our classroom help us create peace and order.
Thank you for the rules that show your love for us.
Help those in charge to
make rules that are for our best. Amen.

Suffering

Have you ever had trouble understanding why something sad happened?

ADAPTED FROM JOB 1:13–20, 22

One day a messenger came to Job and said, "Someone stole your oxen and donkeys and killed your servants." Another came and said, "Fire fell from heaven and burned up the sheep and servants. I alone have escaped to tell you." Another came and said, "Your sons and daughters were eating and drinking at their eldest brother's house, and suddenly a great wind came across the desert, struck the house and it fell on them and they are dead." Then Job arose, tore his robe, shaved his head, and fell on the ground and worshiped. Job did not sin or blame God.

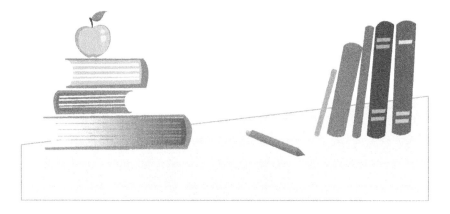

DAY 1

Dear Father in heaven, sometimes things happen
and we don't understand why.
During those times, please help us, Lord.
Help us accept what comes our way.
Help us know you're with us,
especially when times are tough.
Please help us never doubt you and your ways.
Keep us strong so that no matter what,
we know you're holding us close. Amen.

DAY 2

Dear Jesus, you suffered so much.
You suffered for us
because you loved us so much that you died for us.
You suffered because your body hurt
and they did such terrible things to you.
When we're sad and hurting, please help us remember
that you know exactly how we feel
because you felt that way too.
Help us turn to you when we're in pain and need your peace.
Thank you for the comfort of knowing
we can be happy with you in heaven. Amen.

DAY 3

Dear Jesus, you taught us to be strong
when times get tough,
just like you were when you carried your cross.
Even you must have wanted to
lie on the ground after you fell,
but you got up three times.
Help us learn from your example.
When we're sad and hurting, help us be brave like you.
Help us know you'll always help carry our crosses.
Thank you, dear Jesus, for being by our side. Amen.

DAY 4

Dear Holy Spirit, sometimes we can't understand
why bad things happen.
Why do people die? Why can't countries get along?
Why do boys and girls starve?
Why is there war? Why do people hold grudges?
We know we'll never understand everything.
Only God knows the answers to some questions.
O Holy Spirit, fill us with your understanding.
Help us accept what we must
even when we don't understand.
Remind us to pray for others who suffer
and help them know we care about them.
We ask this through Jesus, who suffered for all of us. Amen.

DAY 5

Dear Jesus, it's so hard to watch others suffer.
Sometimes we don't know what to say,
especially when we see others who are lonely, sad, or in pain.
Open our hearts, Lord.
Help us offer comfort with kind words and gentle actions.
May we never turn our backs when someone needs us.
We ask this through you who cared for everyone you met.
Amen.

Holy Week

*Describe a joyful or sad moment
you had this week.*

JOHN 13:1–7

Now before the festival of the Passover, Jesus knew that his hour had come to depart from this world and go to the Father....The devil had already put it into the heart of Judas son of Simon Iscariot to betray him. And during supper Jesus... took off his outer robe, and tied a towel around himself. Then he poured water into a basin and began to wash the disciples' feet and to wipe them with the towel that was tied around him. He came to Simon Peter, who said to him, "Lord, are you going to wash my feet?" Jesus answered, "You do not know now what I am doing, but later you will understand."

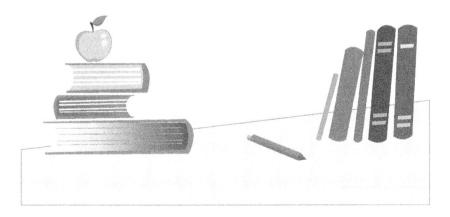

DAY 1

Lord, Jesus, the last week of your life
was filled with many emotions.
Because you were human, you felt pain and fear.
Because you are divine, you had to see it through to the end.
You could have stopped the pain and suffering,
but you loved us so much you said yes.
Thank you for winning life over death for us.
Thank you for overcoming sin and evil for us.
Thank you for opening the gates of heaven
so someday we can be happy with you there. Amen.

DAY 2

Dear Jesus, how happy you must have been on Palm Sunday
when you entered Jerusalem on your donkey.
How happy you must have been
when the excited crowds waved palm leaves.
Thank you for being a king who serves others.
Thank you for being a king who rules with love and not force.
Thank you for being a king who opens his kingdom to everyone.
Thank you for being a king who gave his life for us. Amen.

DAY 3

Dear Lord, on Thursday you celebrated
your Last Supper with your best friends.
You knew your disciples would be sad after you died,
so you gave them two big gifts.
You gave them the gift of bread and wine,
which become your Body and Blood, so we remember you.
You washed their feet to show them we're called to serve.
Thank you, Jesus, for these powerful gifts.
Through them, we find the way to you and your eternal life.
May we always treasure the Eucharist
as the foundation and center of our faith
and as your gift of life in us. Amen.

DAY 4

Dear Jesus, the night before you died
you went to a garden with your apostles to pray.
You asked only that they pray with you,
but they let you down by falling asleep.
Dear Lord, when we let you down, please forgive us.
When we put our needs before yours, please forgive us.
When we're afraid, help us pray like you.
Thank you for showing us
that in all things, we must pray to you, and
that in all things, you'll be there. Amen.

DAY 5

Dear Jesus, what a sad day Good Friday was.
They whipped you, took away your clothes,
crowned you with thorns, and gave you a heavy cross.
Jesus, you carried that cross for *us*.
Help us carry our crosses with love and courage,
as you did yours.
When others try to kill us with their words and actions,
help us be as strong as you were.
Thank you for always being at our side,
sharing in our suffering.
May we help others bear their crosses
by your example. Amen.

Easter

WEEK 41

Resurrection: Alleluia!

*Have you ever felt hopeless about something,
but then it turned out okay?*

MARK 16:1–6

*When the sabbath was over, Mary Magdalene, and Mary the
mother of James, and Salome bought spices, so that they might
go and anoint him. And very early on the first day of the week,
when the sun had risen, they went to the tomb. They had been
saying to one another, 'Who will roll away the stone for us from
the entrance to the tomb?' When they looked up, they saw that
the stone, which was very large, had already been rolled back.
As they entered the tomb, they saw a young man, dressed in a
white robe, sitting on the right side; and they were alarmed. But
he said to them, 'Do not be alarmed; you are looking for Jesus of
Nazareth, who was crucified. He has been raised; he is not here.*

DAY 1

Dear Jesus, It's no wonder
you did what you promised the disciples:
You rose from the dead! Alleluia!!
You keep your promises. We don't keep all of ours.
We say we'll be good, but then we sin.
We say we'll be kind, but we're not.
We know you're there to forgive us when we break our promises.
Please help us keep our promises.
Fill us with your strength
so we always do what we say we will do.
Then *you* can say, *Alleluia, Alleluia, Alleluia*! Amen.

DAY 2

Dear Jesus, sometimes we're just like
the apostles were after you died.
We don't understand why bad things happen to good people.
We get lonely and sad and mad and confused.
We're frustrated when we can't make everything better.
Your resurrection showed us we needn't worry.
We need only put our faith and trust in you.
Help us be strong when we don't understand.
Help us wait patiently until we rise out of our troubles. Amen.

DAY 3

Dear Jesus, your empty tomb
brought joy to the disciples.
They were joyful because you had risen
and come back to life.
They were joyful because they recognized you
on the road to Emmaus.
Help us see you in others and in our world.
May we never be blind to you, and
may we always follow you
out of darkness and into eternal life. Amen.

DAY 4

Dear Jesus, one of your best friends was Mary Magdalene.
She was the first to see your tomb was empty.
She never left your side and always believed in you.
She was the first to spread
the joyful news that you were alive.
You were risen!
Jesus, help us have the same faith in you.
Help us believe in you and never leave your side.
Fill us with your Spirit so
we can proclaim your Good News to others
as Mary Magdalene did.
Then you can call us your loyal disciple.
We ask this in hope. Amen.

DAY 5

Heavenly Father, you sent your son, Jesus,
to Earth to show us how much you loved us.
How happy you must have been
to have him come home to you
when he rose from the dead
and was reunited with you in heaven.
Now heaven is possible for us, because of his love.
Keep us safe and free from harm
until it's our turn to join you in heaven.
Help us spread your message of love just as Jesus did.
We ask this through your Holy Spirit of love. Amen.

New Life

*What habits do you need to let die
or go away?*

JOHN 12:24–26

*Very truly, I tell you, unless a grain of wheat falls into the earth
and dies, it remains just a single grain; but if it dies, it bears
much fruit. Those who love their life lose it, and those who
hate their life in this world will keep it for eternal life. Whoever serves me must follow me, and where I am, there will my
servant be also. Whoever serves me, the Father will honor.*

DAY 1

Dear Lord, you tell us to
be like the grain of wheat—
to die to ourselves so we can grow in you.
Sometimes it's very hard to do that.
We put our own wants and needs before you.
Help us, Lord, to see that we're here
to serve *you* and not ourselves.
Fill us with your love so we can follow you more completely
and enjoy new life with you in heaven. Amen.

DAY 2

Dear Lord, your love is never-ending.
All you ask is that we follow you and put our trust in you.
Sometimes this is hard, Lord,
because we think we're in control.
But, like Jesus, we need to turn our lives
over to you and do your will.
Then we too can have eternal life in heaven.
Help us turn away from our sinful ways and follow you.
We ask this through Jesus, who put his total trust in you.
Amen.

DAY 3

Dear Lord, through your death and resurrection,
you taught us that good comes from suffering.
Help us see that you're still present even when we suffer.
When things are hard for us,
help us be strong like you.
Help us see that we can look to you,
knowing you're sad for us too.
Thank you for always being with us,
offering your love and strength to hold us up
and bear all things. Amen.

DAY 4

Dear Lord, new life is your gift.
New life means we're always
able to start over and that you
always give us second, third, and fourth chances.
Thank you for always forgiving us no matter what we do.
Thank you for placing your Spirit of love within each of us
so we can always be renewed through your love.
Help us see that through life in you,
we can bring life to others.
May we always be living examples of life in you. Amen.

Dear Lord, new life in you means
letting go of old ways of doing things.
Help us leave selfishness, jealousy,
meanness, and dishonesty behind.
Help us see that sharing and being kind and being honest
are ways we can grow in a new life in you.
Help us see that every day we can know you,
love you, and serve you. Amen.

WEEK 43

Divine Mercy

What does it feel like to be peaceful?

JOHN 20:19–23

When it was evening on that day,...and the doors of the house where the disciples had met were locked..., Jesus came and stood among them and said, "Peace be with you." [Then] he showed them his hands and his side....Jesus said to them again, "Peace be with you. As the Father has sent me, so I send you." [Then] he breathed on them and said to them, "Receive the Holy Spirit. If you forgive the sins of any, they are forgiven them; if you retain the sins of any, they are retained."

DAY 1

Dear Jesus, you love us so much
that you gave us a special Sunday
to celebrate your mercy and forgiveness.
You say that *nothing* we have done
will ever make you so mad that you won't forgive us.
Help us remember to ask for your forgiveness
every day as we try to be the best we can be. Amen.

DAY 2

Dear Lord, you appeared to Sister Faustina,
a simple cook and gardener,
and asked her to spread the word and image
of your Divine Mercy.
Even though people didn't believe her, she never gave up.
Help us be like Sister Faustina.
Help us fight for you even when others don't. Amen.

DAY 3

Dear Jesus, you told Sister Faustina
that any soul who strays from your love saddens you.
Help us never stray from you.
Like a shepherd, may you always lead us to you.
Keep us in your care until you lead us home to heaven.
Thank you for being the Good Shepherd. Amen.

DAY 4

Dear Lord, mercy means kindness
and understanding and forgiveness.
Help us forgive one another with that same mercy,
especially in our homes and classrooms.
Thank you for showing us how to love and forgive
so we can be like you. Amen.

Dear Lord, you tell us that no matter what we do,
you will have mercy on us.
Thank you for telling us we should *never* fear coming to you
because of the bad things we have done.
Thank you for pouring forth your healing grace.
Thank you for the peace you give us
in knowing you'll love us always. Amen.

WEEK 44

Gifts of the Spirit

*Tell about a time a gift of the Holy Spirit
came in handy.*

ACTS 2:1–4

*When the day of Pentecost had come, they were all together in
one place. And suddenly from heaven there came a sound like
the rush of a violent wind, and it filled the entire house where
they were sitting. Divided tongues, as of fire, appeared among
them, and a tongue rested on each of them. All of them were
filled with the Holy Spirit and began to speak in other languages,
as the Spirit gave them ability.*

DAY 1

Lord Jesus, we were welcomed
into your kingdom at our baptism.
You strengthened us with water and oil
and anointed us as your children.
Through the gifts of the Holy Spirit,
you strengthen us with special gifts.
Help us remember that you've given each of us
exactly what we need to be closer to you. Amen.

DAY 2

Dear Holy Spirit, we can do great things
through the gifts you bestow on us.
May we live the way Jesus wants us to live.
May we always strive to be the best we can be.
Help us share our gifts wisely.
We ask this through you who strengthen us all. Amen.

DAY 3

Dear Jesus, only through an open heart
can we find our way to you.
Fill our hearts with your love and divine grace.
Open our hearts to the gifts others share with us.
Help us see that when we all use our special gifts *together*,
we can do great things.
We ask this through you, the giver of all things good. Amen.

DAY 4

Dear Holy Spirit, through your gifts
of wisdom and understanding and knowledge,
we see ourselves and others as you see us.
Holy Spirit, strengthen us
and the gifts you graciously bestow on us.
Help us understand that only by learning about you
can we love you more. Amen.

Dear Father in heaven,
how wonderful, how loving, how good you are!
Help us always honor and revere you.
May we always be open to your presence
and be proud to call ourselves your children.
Thanks you for loving us just as we are,
O God of awe and wonder. Amen.

Section 9

We Celebrate

WEEK 45

Mary, Queen of the Universe

What qualities must a queen have?
Did Mary have those qualities?

JOHN 19:25–27

Meanwhile, standing near the cross of Jesus were his mother, and his mother's sister, Mary the wife of Clopas, and Mary Magdalene. When Jesus saw his mother and the disciple whom he loved standing beside her, he said to his mother, 'Woman, here is your son." Then he said to the disciple, "Here is your mother." And from that hour the disciple took her into his own home.

Dear Jesus, how hard it must have been
for you to see your mother
and best friend so sad at the foot of your cross.
Even then, you didn't think of yourself.
You thought about them and tried to bring them comfort.
In your care, you showed us
we should always care about our parents.
Thank you for sharing your
wonderful mother, Mary, with *all* of us.
Thank you for giving us a heavenly mother
to help us with our problems.
All we must do is ask for help.
We ask this through you,
who loved your mom with all your being. Amen.

Dear Jesus, how blessed we are to have two mothers!
You've given us mothers who care for us here on Earth
and *your* mother in heaven,
who cares for us just as she cared for you.
Thank you for the gift of mothers, whose selfless love
gives us a glimpse at how you must love us.
Care for our mothers. Protect them and keep them safe.
Prepare a special place for them in heaven next to your mom
so that someday they too will be happy with you
forever and ever. Amen.

DAY 3

Dear mother Mary, you were so strong
as you stood at the foot of the cross
and watched your only son die.
When we need you to be strong for us,
please be there for us.
When we're sad or weak or hurting
and turn to you for strength, help us be strong.
Ask Jesus to help us be strong.
With you and your Son on our side,
we'll never fail. Amen.

DAY 4

Dear Mary, you lived your whole life saying yes,
even though you didn't know what that would bring.
You said yes to the angel and yes to God.
How hard it must have been to say yes
to Jesus when he died in your arms.
Your faith gave you the strength to say yes.
Help us know that by saying yes, we can be like you.
Thank you for being our model of faith. Amen.

DAY 5

Dear Mary, you showed that true faith
shows willingness to let God take control.
It's saying, "God, work through me."
Mary, thank you for letting God work through you.
Thank you for being a queen who wasn't interested in power,
but in love for everyone.
Thank you for teaching us that love is selfless,
that it's about others.
We love you and honor you. We thank you!
You're the best mother we could imagine.
We can't wait to meet you someday in heaven. Amen.

Spring

*What bad vines or habits do you need
to prune this spring?*

JOHN 15:1–2, 4–5

I am the true vine, and my Father is the vine-grower. He removes every branch in me that bears no fruit. Every branch that bears fruit he prunes to make it bear more fruit....Abide in me as I abide in you. Just as the branch cannot bear fruit by itself unless it abides in the vine, neither can you unless you abide in me. I am the vine, you are the branches.

DAY 1

Dear Jesus, thank you for being a strong and steadfast vine.
Thank you for always being firmly rooted
so we can hang on to you.
Thank you for your bushy branches,
which nourish us so we can
produce your Spirit fruits of kindness,
generosity, and goodness.
Help us become the biggest and best branches we can
to produce our best fruits.
After growing in you, may we enjoy heaven with you. Amen.

DAY 2

Dear Jesus, you are an *awesome* gardener.
You send us what we need to grow:
sun and rain and soft winds, rich soil to bloom in.
Thank you for caring for us
so we can grow to be strong and productive.
Help us bloom where you plant us.
Thank you, dear Jesus, for tending us with love. Amen.

DAY 3

Dear Lord, sometimes we're like a garden
whose old, dead plants must be removed.
We must remove our old habits so new ones can grow.
Help us see that if we don't prune our old vines,
they become overgrown and ugly and wild.
Open our eyes so we can see what we need to prune.
Help us remove bad habits and selfish ways
so new habits can grow.
Prune, trim, clip, and shape us
so we become the most beautiful plants
in your garden. Amen.

DAY 4

Dear Lord, springtime is a season
of hope and joy after a long dreary winter.
Spring replaces the bleakness
of the dead and dormant.
Thank you for springtimes, Lord.
Thank you for giving us joyful moments of hope
to replace the sad and dreary times.
Thank you for all that is new,
for showing us that
we too will be resurrected with you in death
and join you in the eternal life of heaven.
We ask this through Jesus, the hope of the world. Amen.

Dear God in heaven, we love sunflowers
because they're bright and beautiful.
Standing straight and tall, they turn to follow the sun.
We thank you for the gift of your son, Jesus.
Help us be just like sunflowers.
May we always stand straight and tall
and turn toward your Son.
May we be bright and beautiful
because we are filled with life in him.
May we always follow him
no matter what direction he faces
so that others may see us and follow him too.
We ask this of you, Father of all corners of the Earth. Amen.

WEEK 47

Graduation

*How have you changed since
you started school?*

DANIEL 12:3

*Those who are wise shall shine like the brightness of the sky,
and those who lead many to righteousness, like the stars for
ever and ever.*

DAY 1

Dear heavenly Father, education
gives us opportunities to grow
in your love and in knowledge of your gifts.
Education isn't a reality for everyone.
We're so blessed to have not only schools to learn in,
but also the supplies we need and teachers to teach us.
Thank you for giving us minds for learning, eyes for seeing,
and hands for carrying out the lessons we've learned.
May we always use them to serve you. Amen.

DAY 2

Dear Holy Spirit, education and growth
is about making good decisions.
Spirit of wisdom, help us move forward.
Help us use what we've learned to
make good decisions based on what we know about you.
Help our decisions always reflect our love for you,
and may we always make decisions
for the good of all your children.
May we always be examples of your love
so you're proud of us, your children. Amen.

DAY 3

Dear Lord, education fills our minds
with wonderful facts about you and your world
and gives us the opportunity to make many new friends.
As we move forward, Lord, bless us
and bless the friends we've made.
Help us value the gift of their friendship.
Help us too, Lord, to choose new friends wisely,
because they are so important.
Help us make friends who will be a positive influence on us
and friends who will help us grow closer to you.
We ask this through you who chose your friends wisely. Amen.

DAY 4

Dear Lord, our education was possible because
of many important people.
We thank you for our parents,
who brought us to you in baptism,
were our first teachers,
and brought us to this school.
We thank our administrators, who help us pray
and guide us to be the best we can be.
Thank you for their patience, their guidance, their creativity,
their compassion, their wisdom, and their love of learning.
May we always use what we've learned
to the best of our ability. Amen.

DAY 5

Dear Lord, graduation means
opportunities to grow in new ways.
We can grow in wisdom and knowledge,
we can grow in maturity,
and we can grow in love for you.
Lord, help us see that all new opportunities
are gifts from you—
ways we can use the knowledge we've gained,
ways we can grow in new learning.
Above all, guide us to serve you and others
as children of your love. Amen.

End of the Year

Name something you learned this year.

1 JOHN 1–3

What was from the beginning, what we have heard, what we have seen with our eyes, what we have looked at and touched with our hands, concerning the word of life—this life was revealed, and we have seen it and testify to it, and declare to you the eternal life that was with the Father and was revealed to us—we declare to you what we have seen and heard so that you also may have fellowship with us; and truly our fellowship is with the Father and with his Son Jesus Christ.

DAY 1

Dear Jesus, you know how happy
and sad change can be.
You know how hard it is to say goodbye to your friends,
and you know how hard it is to leave what is familiar.
Help us be as strong as you were
when it was time to leave your friends
and join your Father in heaven.
You showed us that even though change is difficult,
it's worth the hardship.
Thank you for filling us with your Spirit
so we can be strong like you. Amen.

DAY 2

Dear Jesus, how exciting it is
to have an entire summer ahead of us!
We'll have time to enjoy our families,
create new memories, learn new things.
Help us, Lord, to be thankful for the memories from this year
and to thank you for the opportunity to learn new things.
Bless our teachers and our classmates,
and keep them safe over the summer.
Keep us safe as we enjoy the outdoors.
Help us make each new day a time
to learn new things and be closer to you. Amen.

DAY 3

Dear Jesus, sometimes it's easy to be lazy in the summer.
We don't have homework, our schedules are easier,
and we have time to do what we want.
Help us see that time is a gift we're called to use wisely.
Help us remember what we learned this year,
to nurture the friendships we made,
to be good helpers around the house and yard,
and to see every moment as a prayer
if we offer it up to you. Amen.

DAY 4

Dear Jesus, vacations are wonderful!
We vacate our regular lives and
fill them with new things,
experiences, and memories.
Thank you for vacations, Lord, but help us remember
that we must never vacate our lives of you.
No matter where we go and what we do,
may we always keep you as our tour guide.
With you in charge, we'll never get lost.
Fill us with your joy as we start our summer vacation. Amen.

Dear heavenly Father, when we're on vacation,
sometimes we think only about ourselves
and what we want to do.
Open our minds and hearts this summer
to see what others need.
Guide our hands and our actions
to be doers of your Word in all ways.
May we see ways to help our busy parents.
May we see ways to help our brothers and sisters.
And may we see ways to help our neighbors.
Thank you for the opportunity to serve you by serving others.
We ask this through you, the best servant of all. Amen.

Prayers For Various Occasions

CLASSROOM BLESSING

Dear heavenly Father, bless our classroom
and the students who learn here.
Fill their minds with the gifts of understanding
so they can absorb and learn.
Bless our teachers, who give of themselves so we can learn.
May this classroom be a place of kindness and respect. Amen.

WELCOME A NEW STUDENT

Dear Jesus, be with us as we welcome a new student.
Help us be the best welcoming committee we can be.
Help us be understanding, sensitive,
gentle, and helpful to (*name*).
Help (*her/him*) know (*he/she*) is a gift to our classroom
as (*he/she*) brings (*her/his*) experiences from another school
and broadens our thoughts. Amen.

WELCOME A NEW TEACHER

Dear Jesus, thank you for sending (*name*) to our school.
We're grateful for the gifts and talents (*he/she*) brings.
Help us open our hearts and minds to (*name*)
so we can learn as much as possible from (*him/her*).
Through (*him/her*), may we be closer to you. Amen.

100 DAYS OF SCHOOL

100 days of school is a lot of school!
Lord, thank you for 100 days to learn about you
and for 100 days to learn about your world.
As we count down to the final days of the year,
fill us with knowledge and help us learn more about you
so we can grow in your love. Amen.

ON A PATRONAL FEAST

Thank you for the gift of saints.
Help us follow their examples of holiness.
Help us respect our names and those we're named after
so we will be living models of their lives. Amen.

BLESSING OF ANIMALS

Dear Lord, thank you for our pets.
For tails that wag and tongues that lick,
whiskers that tickle, and fins that glide, we thank you.
For the squawks and squeaks that fill our homes, we thank you.
Help us care for them as lovingly as you care for us. Amen.

BEFORE AN ATHLETIC EVENT

Dear Lord, strengthen me today as I compete.
Strengthen my body to do the best it can.
Strengthen my mind to help me stay in the game.
Strengthen my heart to accept the outcome.
Help me remember that trying my best
is the most important prize of all. Amen.

BEFORE A MUSIC EVENT

Heavenly Father, thank you for the beautiful gift of music.
May our joyful noise be music to your ears.
We ask that you bless the musicians, their teachers,
and all who will hear their performance. Amen.

BEFORE AN EXAM

Dear Lord, be with us as we take this exam.
Give us patience to focus and answer questions
clearly and completely.
Help us be honest, to value our work,
and to know that all knowledge is a gift from you. Amen.

RECEIVING GRADES

Dear Lord, today is grades day.
This day may fill us with joy, relief, or anxiety.
Celebrate with us as we see the fruits of our hard work.
Give us the strength to continue our studies,
you who are the source of all knowledge
and all things good. Amen.

BEFORE A DANCE OR PARTY

Dear Jesus, you loved to have fun with your friends.
Help us be welcoming and to include *everyone* in our fun.
Help us make wise choices and show our maturity
by acting as you would in strength of character.
Bless all who help us dance
and laugh and make a joyful noise for you! Amen.

BIRTHDAY BLESSING

Dear Jesus, thank you for the gifts of birthdays
so we can honor our friend (*name*).
May the candles on (*his/her*) cake remind (*him/her*)
that (*he/she*) has the ability to spread your light to others.
Protect (*name*) and watch over (*him/her*) always. Amen.

VALENTINE'S DAY

Dear God, thank you for the gift of Saint Valentine.
Help us remember to express our love every day of the year.
We thank you for Jesus, who loves us best of *all*. Amen.

SAINT PATRICK'S DAY

Dear Saint Patrick, thank you for teaching us about bravery
through your fight for freedom.
Thank you for teaching us to appreciate all cultures.
Thank you for teaching us about the Trinity
through the symbol of the shamrock. Amen.

HALLOWEEN

Dear Jesus, thank you for the generosity of those
who give us candy and treats.
Help us respect one another and
the homes where we trick or treat.
Keep us safe as we travel from home to home. Amen.

BURYING THE ALLELUIA

Dear Jesus, today we bury our Alleluias.
Over the next forty days we find no joy
in knowing the suffering you endured for us.
Help us prepare our hearts for you
so that on Easter Sunday we may once again
be joyful of your victory over death.
May we come to know you better
by sharing your pain through the forty days of Lent. Amen.

BEFORE A MEAL

Dear Lord, thank you for the food we're about to eat.
Thank you for your generosity to our bodies and our souls.
Help us to never forget to give you thanks
for giving us what we need.
Bless those who grew this food, those who
harvested it, and those who prepared it.
Be with boys and girls and the parents
who do not have a meal today.
May they find nourishment in their faith in you. Amen.

PRAYER FOR A SICK CHILD

Dear Jesus, healer of all,
please bless (*name*) and all your sick children.
Comfort them in their pain and suffering
so they know they can always find support in you.
Help us aid them any way we can.
May we never take our own health for granted.
We ask this through Jesus, who heals us all. Amen.

PRAYER FOR PARENTS

Dear Father in heaven, we thank you for our parents.
They love us and care for us and protect us from danger.
They are our living sign of how you love us too.
Fill our parents with your Spirit
so they can guide us and lead us to you.
Help them always act in our best interest
and know how much we love and appreciate them. Amen.

GRANDPARENTS DAY

Dear Lord, we thank you for our grandparents.
Thank you for their never-ending love and support,
their wisdom and guidance, and their time.
Help us be patient and appreciate them.
Help us show them how much we love and respect them.
May you keep them in your loving care,
watching over them always. Amen.

LOSS AND GRIEF

Dear Lord, even though we know (*name*) is with you,
we're sad for ourselves.
Jesus, please fill the hole in our hearts with your love.
Comfort us with your peace, and help us understand
that the memories of (*name*) will help ease our loss.
Wrap your arms around us and keep us close to you
as every day we try to recover from our loss. Amen.

TIME OF TRAGEDY

Dear Lord, it's hard to understand why bad things happen.
Help us understand these tragic events,
and help us have faith in you.
Stay by our side as we make our way through this time.
Keep us focused on you. Amen.

MILITARY SERVICE

Dear Jesus, thank you for those who serve in our military.
Thank you for their gifts of bravery and selflessness.
Heal their pains and hurts and fill them with your peace.
May we always be grateful for the gift of freedom.
We ask this through Jesus,
who fought the battle of good over evil just for us. Amen.

FAREWELL TO A STUDENT

Dear Lord, thank you for the gift of (*name*).
May (*name*) go forth from here
with the joy of the friendships (*he/she*) has made
and the comfort of knowing
wherever (*he/she*) goes, (*he/she*) is never alone.
Bless the memories (*name*) carries of this time with us,
and give (*him/her*) courage to go forth
confidently to make new friends. Amen.

FAREWELL TO A TEACHER

Heavenly Father, we thank you for the gift of (*name*).
Thank you for the knowledge (*he/she*) has given us.
Help (*him/her*) know that wherever (*he/she*) goes,
a part of us goes along, too.
May you always keep (*name*) under your wing,
gently guiding and protecting (*him/her*)
to eternal life with you. Amen.

CPSIA information can be obtained
at www.ICGtesting.com
Printed in the USA
BVOW10s1207141117

500389BV00018B/931/P